I WANT

Roland DeCarra

Roland DeCarra was born in Epsom, Surrey, England. After leaving school he worked as a draughtsman for various engineering establishments, Government agencies and the Metropolitan Police.

He currently lives in Dorking, Surrey, England.

In memory of Lacey.

Contents

Acknowledgements

Firstly, I would like to say a big thank-you to everyone at Acorn Independent Press, London, for all their help in finally getting this project into print.

To Clive Reid, Emma Tilley, Albina Francis and Debbie Coombes for reviewing early draughts of this book and for giving me the encouragement to carry-on writing.

Also to Dee Blick from The Marketing Gym Ltd. Horsham, West Sussex for steering me in the right direction.

And to Adobe.com for the usage of the cover image

1

Monday, Work

My bloody alarm-clock clicks into action at 7am making me jolt and buzzes merrily away to itself.

I was partially awake anyway, the result of too much vodka yesterday I'm guessing? I must stop doing that; it always seems to have an adverse effect on me. As soon as my head hits the pillow I'm out for the count only for me to wake up really early the following morning, usually around 4 or 5am just as I did this morning, which is a real pain in the arse as I then spend the following few hours tossing and turning coupled with far too much thinking, along with short spontaneous vivid dreams that usually involve me being naked in some weird situation or another! I guess that's half my problem - I think too much.

I lay here for a couple of minutes in disbelief that the weekend has gone so quickly yet again, listening to the traffic out on the main road - humans going to work. Lacey, my cat, jumps up onto the bed and reaches out one of her paws to me and gently touches my face to say

"Hello". She's a funny old thing, as I stroke her she flops down onto the duvet and stretches out really long and starts purring like mad. There's a lot going on in that little head of hers. I know exactly what she wants though - feeding - again. She's getting far too fat, especially as her belly has started to sag more noticeably now due to her age. Poor old moggy, I hate leaving her in the flat on her own all day while I'm at work but it can't be helped, that's the situation.

Oh well, I guess I have to scrape myself out of bed and face the World, after one long stretch and a click of my toes as I do every morning. I slide my cotton towelling robe from the White Company on over my naked body and head to the bathroom for a pee and to clean my teeth. I always like to sleep naked as much as possible, except of course for those times when my little friend decides to make her monthly call!

Lacey follows me into the kitchen, zigzagging between my bare feet as I walk, almost tripping me up. I click on the kettle and it starts to make a strange noise - no water. I fill it to a quarter-full and try again and it makes a swishing sound as it now starts to boil properly.

I get a half-full bottle of milk and a packet of cat food out of the fridge and have a little smile to myself as I feed my cat, the cause being that I always without thinking seem to feed her before I do myself. I make a cup of tea and two slices of toast with loads of butter and marmalade and then sit myself down in the living-room to watch the early morning news on the TV. It's the same old crap as per usual - a bomb has gone off in the Middle East, failing immigration control, some poisonous Union planning yet another strike and holding the country to ransom with their blinkered Left-Wing bullshit, someone stabbed to death in London, a crash on the M25 with the obligatory tailback (both ways!), and some stupid so-called celebrity bitch with her latest black footballer boyfriend blah blah blah. All in all a sick bloody mess of doom and gloom, depression, recession, anger and hate.

I finish my breakfast, watch the weather forecast - surprisingly it's not raining! - and then head off for a quick shower. I strip and check myself out in the full-length mirror and I'm looking pretty bloody good for a Monday morning, although I do notice that I need to depilate as I can detect some feint stubble; I always like to keep myself smooth and fresh. I really don't have time to do it now or I'll be late for work so that's a job for later.

The water splashes against my naked body and it feels lovely and warm and totally anti-Monday. I don't bother to wash my hair as I'm short of time as I've already said, and anyway it looks okay. After patting myself dry with one of my white Egyptian towels I dress for work. I always pick out what I'm going to wear the previous evening to save time and hassle the following morning.

Today I'm wearing a grey knee-length pencil-skirt and a nicely-cut white cotton blouse, both from H&M, which has a low front as I like to show the World what I've got. Well, you know the old saying - "If you look good, you feel good". And I look bloody fantastic so you can guess how I feel right? I know I'm vain but I have the right to be - I'm gorgeous! Underneath I'm wearing a matching white lacy bra and knickers from Ultimo. On my feet I'm going to wear my grey suede heals from New Look as they're not too high and don't hurt my feet.

After brushing my teeth for the second time I spend about 20-minutes or so putting on some light make-up, nothing too heavy as it's only for crappy work. I tend to use Rimmel London as it suits both my skin and complexion. I add a few squirts of *Luxe* by Avon and with that I'm all done, I look like an angel - a white angel - and I'm now ready to face the World.

I am conscious of trying to be different. Why the Hell should I be like everyone else? Why would I want to be like you?

I give Lacey a cuddle and a kiss goodbye; grab my car keys, lunch box and my clutch bag - a bicolour maxi one from Mango - leave the flat and head to my car - an electric-white Ford Fiesta ST, itself an important extension of my overall freedom.

The drive to work is only a distance of 9-miles or so. I stop off at the local newsagent to get my usual newspaper, its headlines featuring the same stupid bitch that was on the TV news this morning with her bloody black boyfriend, the football player. In this day and age this sort of crap takes precedent over people being killed by bombs or even the state of the economy, which is typical. Are we so dumbed-down in this Country that we now accept this sort of shit first by the media? We live in a World where a nurse earns 20-grand a year for saving lives whilst a footballer gets 100-grand a week for kicking a ball. How is this possible? Everything is upside-down.

Back in the car I make my way down the road, looking at my fellow humans as they walk along the pavement on either side. It's always the same people, all in exactly the same place at exactly the same time every bloody day, day in day out. I spot the old woman in her 60's hobbling along on crutches, the old man whizzing along on his mobility scooter, the middle-aged blonde woman with her mobile phone permanently welded to her ear, the black guy with his loaf of bread (why does he need a loaf of bread every day?), the same school kids in the same place every morning, the really fat guy unloading boxes from his people-carrier and taking them into the local pub, the guys in their suits - the middle-managers and the pen-pushers, all looking exactly the same - like clones. Another old man, a total mess, pissed as a fart and it's not even 9am yet. He might be free as a bird but he's trapped in his own World of alcohol-infused pain. There're all there as regular as clockwork, all stuck in their own little lives.

As you can no doubt tell, I'm very observant. I notice things, not just those men and women who look at me and wonder who I am, but also my surroundings - houses, trees, roads, cars, the wind, air, everything.

Out onto the main road - the A24 - I look at the faces of the drivers coming in the opposite direction to me, all with their blank expressions. They too are all in a World of their own, all driving along on automatic- pilot.

I quickly notice that for some reason the traffic is fairly light for this time of day? There's probably an accident or some kind of hold-up somewhere and that's why there are fewer cars travelling in my direction - South.

In my rear-view mirror I spot that idiot again in his white Audi A3 getting closer and closer to the back of my car. This is the third bloody time this month I've had to contend with this twat driving as close to my rear bumper as he can. Well not today. I press the accelerator to the floor and leave him for dead - laugh it up clown!

I can see his face in my mirror about to burst at any moment because he's been beaten by a girl, what a tosser!

why do men have to be such shits?

***

I arrive at work still with 10-minutes to go. A quick flick through my newspaper to kill some time reveals absolutely nothing.

Oh well, here we go again, the start of another week at this stupid company with these stupid people. Each and every one of them is an absolute anathema to me. The owner of the company - or "The Fat Controller" as I call him! - doesn't even know my name. He always has a good look at my body though, especially my tits! That's whenever he decides to grace my department with his presence of course - at the most once or twice a year! - as he breezes through the office.

I actually used to quite like this job when I first joined the company but not now, the work has changed somehow? The people have also changed and more importantly, I've changed to. I'm not sure I can actually put up with this crap for much longer, I have just about had enough. There simply has to be a better way to make a living than this, hasn't there?

I clock-in and make my way to my section and my desk, sit my bum down, have a yawn and turn on my computer. Even though it's still not time to start work yet, my bloody phone begins to ring with my first customer of the week.

Joan - the office bore - wanders in and sits down at her desk. She must be at least 104-years old! Despite it being a nice warm morning she's wearing a big woolly jumper, coat, hat and gloves! What is wrong with her? We used to speak to each other when I first joined the company, almost like friends really, then all of a sudden she stopped talking to me overnight about eighteen-months ago for some peculiar reason? I don't know why and to be honest I don't bloody care. Life's too short to worry about crap like that. Although there's work to be done it usually takes her a good 20-minutes to actually do something -

lazy old cow. Having said that, she only works about 50% of the day anyway as she's forever yakking-on to anyone who dares to listen to her incoherent mind-numbing crap. She's forever stating the bloody obvious, with endless tales of life during the War and the bloody cost of everything when you convert it back to shillings and pence. Who cares about any of that old shit anymore? I'd really love to tell that old bitch to shut the fuck up with her verbal diarrhoea and her endless pearls of wisdom but I can't, unfortunately I need this job.

It's not just the banter; it's her fucking plumy voice that really gets on my tits. Once it gets into my head it starts rattling around inside I can't get it out, its like a maggot. If she's not nattering then another of her skives is to keep disappearing for a good 10-minutes or so at a time, or even just to sit there and do nothing but stare into space.

She swears she suffers from Bi-Polar Disorder or some such bollocks but in reality she's just a lazy bitch. What exactly has she got to moan about in life anyway? She's got her health - the most important thing - so why does she have to keep moaning about inconsequential shit like her non-existent aches and pains all the time? It's not exactly lung cancer or a brain haemorrhage is it? Bloody hypochondriac.

When she dies I'm going to jump into her grave and pee on her coffin! She'll never die though, I'm never that lucky!

You might be wondering what Inga, my section supervisor, has to say about Joan's lack of commitment to her work but that's the frustrating thing, she doesn't do anything or seem to care or even see what I see? As for Inga herself, she's in her late-60's and with problems of her own, that being she's a chain-smoking pill-popping junkie. There's also a big question-mark hanging over her at the moment regarding her imminent retirement, as in when is she finally going to go? The soon the better I hope, this place actually runs much smoother when she's not here anyway.

There's also the question of course as to who is going to take over the running of the section when she eventually does piss off? I've thought long and hard about putting in for the position myself but I keep asking myself do I actually want the job? I know it's more money and everything but it's also a lot more hassle. If I did take it that bitch Joan would be straight out the bloody door and no mistake!

I look at my watch - a white-faced Sekonda chronograph with matching strap that was a present from Mum on my eighteenth birthday - and notice that it's not even 10am yet. This is going to be one of those long drawn-out days, I can just feel it. How can I possibly be so bored? How on Earth did I end up doing this shit just to make ends meet, wasting my natural talent, wasting my life away?

I take another order on the phone through my headset and another 5-minutes of my life disappears that I will never see again.

I suddenly feel a pair of eyes boring into me and I look around to see it's Inga, the matriarch supervisor, trying to stare me out. Stupid old cow, I wouldn't give her the drippings off my nose! She doesn't even deserve to smell my shit! How dare she try to pilfer my sanity, I've got my own agenda to work to without having her in my head. She had better not underestimate me or I will take her out. If she wants to play psychological mind-games or fire supercilious questions at me then bring it on because she's going to lose, the old bag.

Destroyed.

There are other people around me in the office of course, also taking phone orders, and not a single one of them has any nous at all. They all look like lambs being led to the slaughter. They're such a bunch of hypocrites, all stabbing each other in the back one minute and then licking each other's arses the next.

First of all there's Judy, the office sycophant and total snitch. She's in her early-50's I would say, a little round woman with a round face and rosy cheeks. If you say anything to her she immediately grasses you up to you-know-who. It makes me wonder if these people have anything else to do in life?

Don't they have lives of their own instead of worrying about what other people think and do all the bloody time? Why do they spend so much effort gossiping about shit? Some of these people are twice my age and yet they don't know their arses from their elbows. They just don't seem to have the savvy to do anything at all. They have absolutely no sense of reality, whatever that is? Why do they have to be so bloody annoying? I don't annoy anyone so why do they do it to me?

In the far corner facing me sits Andrea, the tree-hugging Bible-basher, wasting her time praying to the redundant effigy that is her God. I think she's about my age but looks way older, mainly due to the size of her, she must be a 16 or 18 or even bigger? The terrible frumpy outfits she attempts to squeeze into are something else. Why is it that really fat women think they look good in tight leggings when in fact their legs and arses look like sacks full of potatoes? It's just not right.

I really can't understand this God-bothering stuff either, what is it all for? What's it all about? To my way of thinking religion is for the weak-minded who cannot withstand the rigours of everyday life. Can't these people think for themselves? Don't these people have brains?

Next to her sits Thelma, the 40-year old virgin, or "Miss Frigid" as I call her. I don't think I've ever met anyone so plain. How can anyone be so fucking boring? She has absolutely no interest in anything - no hobbies, no sport, nothing. If you don't do anything with your life then what's the bloody point of being alive?

Apparently she still lives at home with her aged parents. Her mother is said to be in her mid-eighties and still cooks for her, makes her a packed-lunch every day and runs around after her like she's still 5-years old! The old dear probably tucks her in at night as well! Bless!

She has absolutely no sense of style either, probably because of her big fat arse! She always seems to wear tight jeans though that makes her look even bigger and causes her thighs to rub together when she walks, which isn't very far by the looks of her! She also has one of those awful haircuts reminiscent of a 1970's crash-helmet! Its fucking terrible!

And talk about an "Old Maid", I don't think she ever seen a cock in her entire life! A prick is not just for peeing through you know woman! One of the guys in the warehouse actually asked her out for a drink one time and she went mental on him, complaining to his supervisor that he had sexually harassed her! Poor sod, he didn't stand a chance. I know everyone has their idiosyncrasies - including myself of course! - but she's just impossible. Why doesn't she sort herself out and do something, like get herself laid for instance?

Next up we have Irenka, the backstabbing Polish bitch, and yet another one with her tongue firmly up the supervisors bum. We've never got on right from day one. She knows I hate her guts, the cow. I wish she would just piss-off back to her own fucking country, bloody immigrant. She knows I can't stand her so that's why she keeps away from me. We don't even bother with the simple pleasantries of saying "Hello" to each other anymore. Just because she's been here longer that me (with this company I mean) doesn't make her my superior in any shape or form. One day I'm really going to have that bitch. It would be a justifiable murder.

On the next work-station sits Rachael, probably the only person in my section that I have any real connection with. I don't have any real friends *per se* as I live a self-induced isolated existence. I'm not interested in Facebook or any of that other social network shit either. Why would I be when I consider myself anti-social? Who would I contact anyway? In reality, at the end of the day, I don't really want to be anti-social but that's what circumstances dictate so that's what I am.

Rachael's a little older than me at thirty-seven. She's a real home-girl type as she still lives with her parents. She does have a boyfriend though – Gary - one of the guys in the marketing department. We usually have our breaks together where we try and put the World straight, although it's not usually that simple as that old bag Joan is always sticking her bloody nose into our conversation. I can't bear to be around these people, that's why I've had to cut the wheat from the chaff and why Rachael is the only real person I talk to here.

Unfortunately there are only two guys in my department. The first one, Graham, a guy in his mid-fifties and unmarried, is a bit of an enigma. He's another strange one, a real pen-pusher type. It's like he exists but at the same time he's not actually there. If he was alone in the office you still wouldn't even notice him as he's so bloody boring! He's the type of guy that probably spends his evenings knocking one out in a sock!

The only other guy in my department is Peter, or "Mr Fucking-Know-It-All" as I've nicknamed him. He's only in his early-20's but thinks he knows everything about everything in life when in fact he knows fuck-all. There's always one bloody smart-arse in every company and this one is a real star. If his head gets any bigger it would fall off his shoulders! There is no subject on this Earth that he's not an expert on, he's such a twat!

For some reason he's managed to get his tongue firmly wedged up the Managing Directors arse. He's always sucking-up to him - probably quite literally! He swans around the office like he owns the fucking place, I really can't stand him.

Probably the worst aspect about him is the smell, he absolutely reeks of B.O. I don't think he's ever had a wash in his entire life! I know some women seem to like that sort of thing but I certainly don't. I always keep a can of air-freshener in my desk draw just in case he happens to walk past me! Wank-stain!

Last but not least there's Jennifer, a strange little EMO-girl in her early-20's who just sits in the corner not speaking to anyone at all throughout the entire day. She looks like a ghost, although I've got a horrible feeling that she's one of those many young girls these days that has a negative-body image. But I could be wrong?

Everyone in the office seems to think that she's a lesbian but so what if she is? If that's her thing then good-luck to her, that's what I say. I can't honestly say it's really my cup of tea but what the Hell? I have thought a couple of times about what it would be like to have sex with another girl but I'm not so sure that I could actually go through with it. I do see several attractive women around with really nice tight bodies and wonder to myself about them, but going any further than that is not really on the cards for me.

As I sit here taking another phone order, I suddenly catch a glimpse of Richard, the company post-boy. He's quite hot but a bit too young for me at only twenty, although I've seen the way he looks at me as I've caught him quite a few times having a cheeky look down my cleavage and also at my bum and my beautiful long legs. He's heading in my direction although I'm trying not to notice him.

He comes and stands right next to me and puts my post in my in-tray. I don't know what aftershave he's using but he smells really lovely and I can feel the small hairs on my arms suddenly spring into life. I turn my head up towards him to say "Thank you" only to find him once again looking at my breasts down the v-shaped opening of my blouse! Cheeky little sod!

Given half the chance he would screw me on my desk right now. Given half the chance I would let him!

By now it's lunchtime and there's a guy that comes into the company car park with his sandwich van. He's a bit on the expensive side so I only use him a couple of times a week at the most, and today I only want a packet of crisps as I've brought my own packed lunch. The guy himself - I can never remember his name! - is about twenty-five or so and a bit on the chubby side, especially around his belly, although he's actually not that bad looking. Whenever I'm in the queue I always know that he's got his eye on me and it makes me feel a bit strange, sort of nervous I guess? He seems like a nice enough guy I suppose but I'm not really interested.

It gives me a real sense of power knowing that there's all these men around me that want to shag me but that it's me that's calling the shots. I'm in total control not only of myself but of them also.

On the way back to the office I pass a gaggle of smokers all puffing away on their fags like their whole lives depend on it, which is totally ironic of course as they're slowly being eaten away from the inside-out by their selfish act. Idiots. What do they look like? They all have the face of the Grim Reaper himself. I steer around them and their foul stench and go back to my desk to eat my sarnie - salmon and cucumber today - and the packet of crisps from the sandwich guy - prawn flavoured - my favourite!

The rest of the day drags on and on in an endless spiral of monotony. I'm so fucking bored it's unbelievable. I look around me and what do I see? Nothing. Nothing exists anymore. Looking at my fellow work colleagues I assume that they too are also trapped. I wonder if any of them actually think about me? I somehow doubt it. As you can see, they're quite an eclectic bunch!

My fantasist mind begins to work overtime as my imagination darts from one crazy thought to another - sex with Richard on my desk right in front of everyone, putting an axe through Joan's head, being tied to a tree all whipped and bloody, getting totally pissed out of my head and running down my High Street naked, shooting that guy with the Audi in the face and other such glorious things.

I am blessed with the strength and power to turn my dreams into reality; the power of alter. I try to snap myself out of my daydream but it's hard as the reality of my surroundings are far worse than my make-believe. I'm seriously starting to think my whole life is turning into one long dream of escapism. Escaping from the here is a dream that has to one day turn into reality. I'm not sitting here doing this shit for the rest of my life, digging my own grave. I hate this job just as I've hated all my previous ones. Each and every one of them has been like a prison sentence, restraining me from living my own life. I know that I'm destined for greater things. There is so much more inside me that wants to come out.

Over time I have learned to ignore my job and the people I work with but it's never that easy. This afternoon there are some visitors coming to look around all the departments, including mine. I think they're some of our own company reps but as per usual us workers never get told anything concrete and are always left in the dark. Anyway, because of the visit everyone has to be on their best behaviour so I have to be a good girl, which obviously goes against my grain.

Preceding the visit all the managers and supervisors have been around checking up on every department to make sure everything is in place, although their artifice doesn't fool me for one second. They're all a bloody joke, scurrying around like headless chickens and for what? A bunch of people who have no real interest in what they're being shown in the first place. What's the bloody point?

Inga soon appears from nowhere with three people in tow, two guys - both in their 50's and both out of condition, and one woman. She's about my age and very smartly dressed in a white blouse and a high waist-banded tan-coloured pencil-skirt and has her hair tied-up in exactly the same way as mine although hers is brunette against my blonde and again, although she is attractive, she's nowhere near as gorgeous as me, she just doesn't have the facial bone-structure for a start.

The three of them look at me with their noses upturned as they waft by my desk expressing their artificial interest, all obviously wondering why someone of my age and looks is stuck here doing this crap? These people will never understand what freedom means, certainly to me. And why on Earth would I want to be like them anyway? Prostituting myself in the name of some uncaring faceless company; and for what, a few extra pounds and a company car? No thank you.

They breeze through the office in a matter of 2-minutes at the most and then disappear. They're probably all off down the pub now to get pissed. The whole thing has been a complete waste of bloody time. So what's new?

The end of the day can't come around soon enough and as sure as eggs are eggs it arrives with a merciful relief. Sounds of packing-up is soon followed by the sound of the buzzer. I clock-out and I'm gone. I have total freedom.

***

On the way home I decide to make a quick stop at the supermarket to have a look around in the clothes section. I spot a lovely cream cardigan for only £14.99 so I buy it; it will look great with nothing on underneath, except a bra of course. I actually feel a little happier now after my bit of retail therapy as I head for home and Lacey.

I arrive back at my flat by 6pm to find her waiting for me, staring out the window. She spots me and says "Hello" and I wave back to her. As I enter my front door I step over a pile of post on the mat, its the usual crap - my bank statement, junk mail, a letter from the vets regarding Lacey's booster injection and a small catalogue from some obscure company that I've never heard of selling ridiculous things that nobody really needs or wants.

I've lived in this flat for almost 5-years now. Before coming here I was living in a similar place in a small South London suburb but in the end it was driving me insane. Not only is London expanding and swallowing up its satellite towns but the massive influx of immigrants, particularly Eastern Europeans, the area I was living in was being reduced to something resembling a shanty-town. When a herd of Bulgarian Gypsies moved in next door to me that was the final straw - I was gone. I put up with their evil bloody Gypsy music playing all bloody night long as well as beer bottles and fag butts being thrown over the fence into my garden for over 18-months until I could take no more.

I contacted the Police but they weren't interested as I assumed they were shit-scared of being branded racist. The Council and my local MP were likewise of the same altitude

- not interested. It's all a crying shame, I really loved that old place but now its been totally destroyed for me. I have been back to the town a couple of times but its just not the same, the English heart has been ripped out of it.

I'm by no means the only one of course that has been affected of course; the amount of "White Flight" throughout England is enormous and will spell disaster in the future for those of us who remain true and loyal to this Country.

Anyway, life goes on and mine certainly does. I wasn't going to let that bloody scum or anyone else ruin my existence and so that's why I moved further South to the Surrey / West Sussex border. One might say that I'm a NIMBY and they would be right, I am, but my back yard is my Country, not just the place I happen to be living in at the present moment. It's a far better quality of living around here than in South London although in the relatively short time I've been here I've already noticed a change in the area as the rot is rapidly creeping further afield. It won't be long before I'll be forced to move once again, further South and to yet another town. Where will it all end?

I give Lacey a kiss and a cuddle and she starts to purr a deep throbbing noise that makes me smile. In the living room I kick off my shoes and switch on the TV and would you bloody believe it? It's the same bloody shit on the news as it was this morning! Maybe it still is this morning and I haven't been to work and I'm stuck in some kind-of "Groundhog Day" scenario? No, that can't be possible, can it?

I've got a bit of a strange feeling in my head which spins a roller-coaster ride of emotions in my mind. I grab a couple of paracetamols from my bedside cabinet and wash them down with a glass of German white wine from the fridge.

For dinner I make myself salad and chips with a few slices of ham, nothing fancy. I give Lacey a few slices also along with her own dinner of some chicken in sauce from its packet, and then plonk myself down in front of the telly with my plate and the remainder of the bottle of wine.

Lacey munches away on her food making a loud slopping noise. She's good company for me as I live alone; my independence means everything to me as I've already explained. I know I've largely ostracised myself socially to some degree through this choice but that's the way my life is. I can't help it, that's the way I am. I'm in complete charge of my life and I make my own decisions. I don't want to end up married and bored to death for the rest of my life!

As I channel-hop I find that there is literally nothing on the TV at all apart from some crappy Australian soaps, numerous antique shows (all of them bloody repeats), a couple of American so-called fly-on-the-wall shows featuring these bloody awful women with their big hair, big mouths, plastic faces and fake breasts who obviously have far too much money and too much time on their bony hands to spend it. After that I count at least ten different jewellery channels selling nothing but tat. It's incredible, just who buys all this crap?

There's also a never ending amount of house-building and renovating programs, all copying and trying to out-do one another, and so-called "Celebrity" reality shows where nothing is actually real. These people seem to spend so much of their time pretending to be someone else that they don't even know who they are themselves anymore.

Finally I find a strange Japanese film to watch so I settle myself down to see that, finish my meal, finish the wine and see the movie to the end. Lacey is by now fast asleep on my lap - bless!

Feeling a whole lot more chilled-out now I decide to have a long hot bath in an attempt to make myself sleep a bit better than I did last night. I run the hot water in the tub and add a couple of cap-full's of peach scented bath soak. Before I jump in though I have to deal with my fanny-stubble first. I like to do this as often as I can but I'm not always in the right mood. I always use a hair dissolving cream with Shea Butter which only takes a few minutes to react and then all I have to do is just wash it off with warm water, leaving me all nice and smooth. It lasts like this for well over a week. I've been shaving my pubic hair ever since I was in my mid-teens but back in those days I always used a twin-bladed razor which was a bit of a chore. Over the years my skin had gotten used to it until I started using the cream which is so much nicer - no more of those nasty bloody nicks or razor bumps!

All smooth and cleaned up I ease myself slowly into the hot water. It stings my undercarriage slightly as they come into contact with one another, although once submerged the water feels glorious over my smooth skin as I slide down into it with the bubbles popping away under my chin. I'm in Heaven.

For some strange reason I've suddenly taken a liking to listening to classical music - I guess I must be getting old! I'm not really into anything heavy as such but I have taken a bit of a shine to some of the more popular pieces like *Finlandia* by Sibelius, *Montagues & Capulets* by Prokofiev, *Carmina Burana O Fortuna* by Karl Orff, *The Flower Duet* by Delibes, *Mars* by Holst, *Adagio from Spartacus* by Khachaturian and many others. But my absolute favourite has got to be *Adagio for Strings* by Samuel Barber, the violin really rips my heart out and it always brings a tear to my eye. I've made a CD that I burned from my computer featuring all of my favourites and so that's what I'm playing now as I soak away the memories of my day in the bath.

Don't get me wrong though, I still love some of the contemporary artists - like my favourites PJ Harvey, The Yeah Yeah Yeahs and the occasional bit of Dido to chill out to - but I think I must be going through a funny phase musically at the moment.

My body feels super-soft when I finally get out of the bath and amazingly not wrinkly at all. My fanny-area looks a bit red from the depilating and the heat from the water but that will soon die down and leave me all lovely and smooth for some while yet. I dry myself off with one of my favourite white Egyptian towels and then put on a robe, the black satin one from Fortnight which makes me shiver when it touches my hot naked skin.

I put the kettle on to make myself a cup of tea - and yes, there is water in it this time! - adding a small amount of milk and 1½- spoonfuls of sugar. Back in the living room I switch on my computer - a Packard Bell laptop in white which is very me! - and check my Emails. I have twenty-three messages, mainly just crap and junk which I don't even bother to read and just delete. I have one from Mum which is typical of her messages, an endless sentence of chat about her bloody neighbours who she assumes I both know and care about but I don't of either.

I also have one from my younger sister Kate who likewise waffles on about subjects that I have absolutely no interest in, for instance her childish so-called boyfriend Mick with whom she can't decide whether to keep seeing or split up with. Stupid cow.

Time always seems to travel at twice the normal speed when I'm on my home computer and before long I realise it's nearing 10.30pm and time for bed. I wish my work computer would have the same time-shifting capabilities instead of inducing me into a bloody coma like it does every day!

I give Lacey her night-time feed, a kiss and a stroke and then hit the sack. I write my thoughts and experiences of the day down in my diary, as I do every day. I've kept one ever since I was a little girl, for some 20-years or so now. With that done I click my reading light off and snuggle down beneath my duvet.

Tomorrow is another day - Tuesday, Work.

2

Shops

I've decided to take a free day today, that's from work of course. In other words I've thrown a sickie. And why the Hell not? I deserve it. My Mum rang me last night wanting to meet up for coffee so that's why I'm bunking-off work. Obviously I can't meet her in my local town just in case I'm spotted by one of my nosey co-workers, so we've arranged to meet up a bit further afield in Chichester, West Sussex.

I arrive in town a bit earlier than our set meeting time so I can have a quick look around the market that's set to one side of the car park off of Market Road. You never know, I might find something I fancy?

It's really warm out today so I've dressed light in a banded cream dress from Misguided - not too short but short enough to show off my beautiful long legs. The dress is also very tight and hugs my figure nicely, especially around my bum and chest and feels really lovely and sexy, as does my underwear, in red lace from Ultimo. Not everyone can be as perfect as me you know!

I really can't stand walking around with a great big bag full of crap on my shoulder so I'm just using a small white leather clutch-bag from Mulberry today, neat and simple. On my feet though I've got a pair of cream-coloured suede platform heals from New Look. Fashion comes before pain in my book!

I've also got my full killer-face on today featuring pink lipstick, dark-grey eye shadow with thick black eyeliner and plenty of blusher to accentuate my high cheekbones. I've tied my hair up in a pony-tail as per usual, which all in all took me bloody ages this morning to get just how I wanted. Today's perfume is *Poison* by Christian Dior.

In the market I buy a giant Art Deco-style hair-clip from a stall run by some horrible looking foreigner, possibly a Turk or a Greek? He stares at my chest as I hand him the £3 for the clip and then make my escape. Bastard.

I'm supposed to meet Mum in a little Italian coffee bar called *Bela Mocha* in South Street. It's a lot quieter down this road away from all the hustle and bustle of East Street, that being the main High Street in the town. When I arrive there I notice that I'm early and that she's late - both situations as per usual. I've noticed this becoming more apparent in her as she gets older, although I guess it has to be expected really doesn't it?

I order a Latte from the young girl waitress - not English, probably yet another bloody Pole? - and I sit outside watching the World go by as I wait for Mum. My coffee arrives quickly and tastes lovely as I take a couple of small sips. I watch the faces of people walking by me, some looking seemingly happy whilst others are as miserable as sin. Most though have an expression of indifference. They're all going about their own way in their individual little Worlds.

An old lady of about eighty shuffles by, her face a mass of deep lines. We look and smile at each other and I wonder what she's thinking? Is she thinking about me? Is she looking at me and remembering her own life when she was my age? Is she looking at my tight figure in envy or in some other way, like in admiration or something? I wonder what she looked like at thirty-two? Is she my future self or am I her past? Maybe it's both? I soon spot Mum on the other side of the road heading in my direction, frantically waving at me and so I give her a little wave back. Every time I see her I notice how much older she's looking and it somehow frightens me. It's like she's actually decaying right before my very eyes.

"You look thinner and thinner every time I see you", she says, as she does every time, sitting herself down opposite me without a mention of the word "Hello" or even to enquire if I'm okay?

"Mum, I'm fine. Don't start on me already", I snap back at her.

"I'm not going on at you, I'm just saying", comes back her reply, closely followed by one of my own.

"Well don't then", nipping her side of the conversation in the bud, thus avoiding one of her endless condescending lectures where she always makes a mountain out of a bloody mole-hill.

The foreign waitress suddenly reappears from nowhere and asks Mum what she would like to order.

"A coffee please", she says back.

"Mum, you have to be a bit more specific. Like a Cappuccino or a Latte like the one I have", I calmly inform her.

"Oh I see. I'll have a Latte then please", she says to the girl who then trots off back into the bar.

The forthcoming conversation winds its way around and about the usual tired old routes featuring the same tired old subjects:

"Any new boyfriend on the scene?", "How's the cat?", "How's the car?", "How's work?", "Are you alright for money?"

I know she means well but sometimes I really wish she would just back off. I've even seriously contemplated having her mouth wired shut! I really do love her, in my own unique way, and I absolutely dread her leaving me, which I know one day she inevitably will.

My mobile suddenly rings and catches me by surprise. It's work, checking up on me no doubt. I let it ring, refusing to answer them as they will undoubtedly pick up on the background noise of the traffic on the street and then I'll be for it.

"Well, aren't you going to answer it?", Mum says sharply in her usual somewhat patronising tone.

"Oh, it's no-one important", I bounce back at her.

Mum looks at me the way she does when she wants me to open my life up too her but I shut the door in her face. If I did tell her about my entire life, about every little thing that I get up to, she would never speak to me ever again. I even have secrets from myself.

The conversation turns to my sister Kate and her idiot boyfriend, or "Mr. Useless" as I call him. It turns out he's just got the sack once again for the umpteenth time after being at his new job for only 3-days! Twat!

As I sit there half-listening to all this crap I become distracted by visions of my life, including an image of my own naked body, which I adore more than anything. Mum soon recognises that I'm not listening to her anymore but she still rattles-on regardless about me getting married and having kids and all that old shit. I can't stand anymore of this and suddenly spring back into life, telling her in no uncertain terms:

"Mum, I am quite capable of living my own life you know."

"I know you are but I'm just saying", comes back the same tired old reply.

I like being a loner and living a single life so why can't people just accept that?

Alone, that's a fucking joke. I've been alone all my life. If I was in a room with a thousand people I'd still be alone. Even when I'm having sex with some guy I'm still alone. I have more loneliness than any normal person can withstand. I am never truly happy.

Why is it there always seems to be this weird peer-pressure from family, friends and especially the media about getting married, having kids, a mortgage and all that old bull? None of this stuff is for me at this stage of my life. Maybe in the future things will be different, who knows? I am only thirty-two after all? What's the big rush? I know my biological clock is ticking away but at the end of the day it's my life and I'll live it how I please. I don't class myself as being unconventional; I class myself as being free and individual and above all, being me. You cannot count on anyone in life, not even your parents. That's why I will always try and lead this individual existence of mine and if that makes me an outcast in most people's eyes then so be it.

With both our coffee's drunk and the conversation exhausted, yet another mother / daughter meeting comes to a close. I'm pretty sure that she told me all this stuff on the phone yesterday anyway, I wasn't interested then and I'm certainly not interested now. As per usual the conversation was a one-way affair anyway as she never seems to listen to me even when I do say anything, she never has. If I did actually say something meaningful and she did actually listen to my problems for once I would surely be faced with yet another of her ultimate classic comebacks:

"Well, there are plenty of people who are far worse off than you Sarah."

"No really? You don't say?"

We hug and kiss and wish each other well and then go our separate ways once more. Mum's off to the garden centre whilst I'm off to the shops to treat myself for being such a good girl. Again!

I do love this town; it has a better range of shops than where I live so it was a good call to come here in the first place. I feel like a dog with two-tails. My first port of call is a small upmarket clothes shop called *Kiss Kiss* where I buy a lovely cream v-necked jumper and a crazy pair of blue suede platform court shoes by Lola that are to die for.

Another clothes shop next door is my next target. It's not quite as posh but also has some nice things on display, although as I'm browsing around I sense the feeling that I'm being watched. The two young bitches behind the counter, both around 20-ish, are standing there obviously talking about me. When I turn and stare back at them with daggers they suddenly burst into two simultaneous fake smiles - arseholes. I decide to leave the shop there and then; I'm not letting these couple of cows ruin my bloody day.

What the Hell is wrong with everyone? Is it me or am I being paranoid about everyone looking at me?

As I exit the shop a couple walk by me going in the opposite direction, a man and a woman both in their mid-fifties. The woman stares at me in a strange way but says nothing. My brain immediately goes into overdrive as I suddenly twig where I've seen her before, she works in the packing department at the same

23

company as me. Oh shit, I don't fucking believe it! I just know that she'll bloody grass me up, the bitch, and then I'll be screwed for sure. Then again, why isn't she at work? Maybe she's bunking off as well? It'll just be my bloody luck she isn't though.

I strut my way up the road like the bees-knees I am, exuding my aura of superiority all the way. I come upon a funny little odds and sods shop at the end of East Street; its one of my favourite places to chill-out in town as I always find something in here to cheer myself up.

I wander around lost in my own little World, laughing to myself at some of the weird and wonderful things for sale. I settle upon a fridge-magnet that has the quotation *"Cats Leave Paw Prints on your Heart"* for the princely sum of only £2.99 and a small glass figurine exactly the same colour as Lacey - black with white paws and a white chest - that I just have to buy for the not to unreasonable price of £14.99. Its so sweet!

I pay the bill for my two items and then head back to the car park, cutting through the market, which is far busier now than it was earlier, whilst also making sure to avoid the horrible gaze of the foreigner I bought the hair-clip from. I put my things in the boot of my car and head off back home.

At the edge of town I stop off at the supermarket to do a bit of food shopping. I can't believe how packed the car park is and it takes me a good 10-minutes just to find a space. Grabbing a trolley, one of the shallow smaller ones, I wander around the store looking at stuff to buy. I pick up a nice black v-neck t-shirt that is bound to look good on me, a lovely bottle of sweet German wine (white of course), a bar of chocolate (to go with the wine later), some cat food, tampons, a bag of organic carrots, an organic broccoli and a chicken Jalfrezi curry with rice ready-meal also for later as I can't be bothered to cook tonight.

I stand in line at one of the ordinary tills to pay my bill as I can't abide those bloody do-it-your-self checkouts, they always seem to go wrong every time I go near one! The young girl on the till - I guess she's probably about 18 or so - looks at me and smiles somewhat begrudgingly. I smile back a fake smile of my own and tell her that I would like £50 cash-back on my bill. I usually do this at supermarkets as it saves me having to go to the bank or one of those dodgy ATM machines for cash.

As I load my things into two plastic bags, a quick sideways glance at the checkout girl reveals her having a sneaky look at my two girls! Cheeky cow! I also notice hers which are very small but then again maybe she has time on her side for some improvement? All finished at the checkout I make my way back to the car and load my shopping into the boot with the rest of today's things. Before heading home though, I do a quick stop at the petrol station next door for half a tank of fuel and then I'm away at last.

I head back along the fast stretch of the A27 heading East and put my foot down, screaming past the opposition in their boring crappy cars because that's what I want and because I'm free. If I want to do 130mph in a 70-zone then that's what I'll fucking do. If you don't push yourself then what's the bloody point of being alive?

As I'm tearing along I begin to think about this morning with Mum whinging and whining on about meaningless crap and all the other people I've met and seen so far today. It's a strange old World isn't it? I do a sharp left onto the A29 and head for Bury, pushing on.

At the top of Bury Hill I stop off for a burger with onions and salad and a Coke. I sit in my car as I have my lunch, watching and observing all the people drive and walk past me as I munch away. A guy in his late-forties in full cycling regalia gets his mountain bike out from the back of his van and pedals off into the woods. As he rides past and disappears he looks at me looking at him but neither of us reacts. He's nothing too me and I don't care anyway.

With lunch consumed I continue my journey North down Bury Hill itself and back home to sanctuary, back home to Lacey and my own little World.

***

This afternoon I decide to enjoy myself. I am totally in love with my body and even the very thought of being a free independent young woman turns me on all the time. I down a couple of glasses of the lovely German wine that I bought this morning, saving the rest for later.

In the bathroom I strip naked and look at myself in the full-length mirror and smile as the reflection before me is both beautiful and flawless. I simply cannot believe how gorgeous I am! I touch my right-breast with my left-hand and squeeze it as I push my right-hand between my legs and gently play with my vagina with my fingers. The sensation making me giggle momentarily.

I make my way to my bedroom still with my hand stuck between my thighs and lay down on the bed face-up with my gorgeous long legs apart as wide as they will go. I insert 2-fingers into my body and begin to wank myself off. The effect of the wine quickly fires me up to go faster as I rub my clit with my thumb, increasing with intensity the more I go on.

Oh my God that feels so fucking good!

In only a few seconds I cum, my juices squirting out over my hand and the duvet below as I push myself to the end.

I lay there panting for a short while as I try to let my heartbeat return to some semblance of normality and exhale a deep sigh and smile at myself for being such a good girl. Rolling off the bed I return to the bathroom to clean myself up and then make my way to the airing cupboard in the hallway to get a clean duvet cover.

The rest of the evening runs fairly smoothly. I feed Lacey and myself, have the rest of the bottle of wine, the chocolate and then a large neat vodka or two whilst watching a funny French film on TV followed by a nasty German horror. Later I check my Emails and then watch some hard-core porn on my computer and masturbate once again, this time doing it at my computer desk as I watch lesbian orgy prolapse licking which I find really disgusting but I watch it transfixed anyway.

At 10.35pm I feed Lacey once again, actually for the fourth time today, and then head off to bed.

All in all it's been a pretty good day today I think to myself as I lay in bed staring at the ceiling with Lacey now curled up dozing by my side. I bought some nice things, met Mum for a chin-wag, the Sun was shining, I showed off my figure and turned a few heads therefore making a few people jealous, had a few drinks or six and pleasured myself a couple of times - sweet!

I suppose I must show my face at work tomorrow but I don't really want to think about that shit right now. Maybe my Doctor was right when I went to see her yesterday - I'm over a week late for my dreaded curse – maybe I do have stress like she told me after all?

What stress? The only stress I have is the stress I put myself under by worrying what the future holds for me? That and thinking the whole World is watching me all the bloody time.

Maybe I am paranoid after all?

Maybe I'm not?

3

Car Trouble

I've got my car booked in at the local garage this morning at 8.30am so I've taken the day off work - again!

I don't know what's wrong with it but its been mucking me about all week with the engine misfiring and stuff. How can this be happening, I only had the thing serviced 2-weeks ago? This is just typical, yet more bloody expense.

Anyway, I'm going to drive it down to the garage and then walk back as it's not too far; anyway it'll do me good to get some fresh air into my lungs for a change. Then I'm just going to chill-out for the rest of the day; I think it's good to have a lazy day every now and then don't you, to be away from all the hustle and bustle and all the crap of life?

There's no need to dress up today as I'm not putting myself on show for anyone, I'm only going to the garage after all. I've just thrown on a white v-neck t-shirt from Tu, a pair of blue stone-wash stretch-jeans from Cotton Traders and a matching set of lacy bra and knickers from Triumph underneath. My footwear is a pair of white Addidas trainers from JD Sports seeing as I'm going to walk home. I've just added some light make-up, nothing fancy, as my natural beauty will see me through the day. I've tied my hair up in a pony-tail as per usual so everyone can see my face fully. I've also added a few squirts of *Opium* by Yves Saint Laurent to make myself smell all lovely, just for me of course.

I give Lacey a kiss and stroke the top of her head as she sits on the back of the sofa watching my every move and then I go.

I arrive at the garage in only 5-minutes flat, parking up on their forecourt, and make my way to their reception office. There are two women that man the desk. The first is around 60-ish and grey-haired. She always seems quite nice to me and has a very dry sense of humour, somewhat similar to my own. The other woman is a little younger at around fifty-something. She's equally okay to me but doesn't have the same humour rating. She does have a very impressive cleavage though!

"Hello, how my I help you?" says the one with the chest, who if I remember correctly her name is Clair.

"Hi, I've got my car booked in for 8.30 under the name of Knowles", I tell her.

At that moment Carl, the garage owner and manager, enters the office and his face lights up as soon as he notices me.

"Hello Sarah, how are you?"

"I'm fine thanks and you?" I reply, somewhat over cheerfully.

"Oh, working hard as per usual. So what's wrong with the car?"

"I'm not sure. It doesn't seem right somehow. Its been like it for about a week now", I come back.

"It's probably something simple; I'll get one of the lads on to it. How are you getting back home?" He enquires.

"Oh, it's okay, I'll walk back, it's not far."

"There's no need for that Sarah, I'll drop you back if you like?"

I stand there not knowing which way to turn as I hate having my plans changed for me, no-matter how trivial they are, also wondering where this situation could potentially lead?

Before I can even think straight I suddenly blurt out "Okay then" like a big soppy girl! I guess there's no harm in it anyway and it would save me having to walk all the way home.

"Let's have the keys and then I can see what's wrong with the car as I drive you back."

He smiles at me like a cat that's got the cream as I sheepishly hand him my car keys. We make our way out to my car with Carl getting in behind the wheel with me slipping into the passenger seat. We drive out of the forecourt and head off up the road in the direction on my place. I sit there wondering to myself how he somehow knows exactly where I live?

I would say that Carl is around his mid-forties at a guess. He has one of those shaved heads that I don't really like although he doesn't look thuggish like a lot of guys do, he's actually quite nice looking.

We pull up outside my flat and Carl switches my car's engine off and turns to look at me. I sit there like one of those plastic shop dummies for what seems like an age as then suddenly I now realise where this situation is going and my throat takes a small gulp to itself.

Have I read the signals right? Am I barking up the wrong tree? What signals have I been sending out? Do I have that look on my face that women get when they are attracted to a guy or when they're on the come-on? What is this strange phenomenon that keeps creeping up on me and makes me do wild things? I know I'm always horny but this is crazy!

In total silence Carl leans over to me and touches my left-cheek with his right-hand. He guides me closer to him and I respond just as you would expect me to and we kiss passionately.

What the Hell am I doing? What a stupid question, I know exactly what I'm fucking doing but why am I doing it? It's another stupid question,

I'm doing it because I want him - right now. I break away from him with the words:

"Are you coming in or not?"

Once inside my flat we stand and stare at each other for a moment in the hallway. We both know that we've now reached the point of no return. This is bloody madness! I simply do not know anything about this guy but I do know that I want him to screw me right here and now. I don't even know if he's married or not? I suspect he is although he doesn't have a ring on his finger. I just don't care anyway. He might even have kids for all I know? All these questions are irrelevant too me right now as all I want is him inside me.

The adrenalin pumping through my body reaches a thousand-miles-an-hour and makings me dizzy with excitement. My head has gone almost weightless and my breathing has doubled its pace. I notice my breasts heaving as I try in vain to take in more air but it's no use, I've lost control.

I lunge myself at him and physically pull him towards me. We kiss hard as he runs his hands over my back and it feels so good that I want him to hold me in his arms forever, protecting me from this nasty World. My right-hand is on his back but I soon let go with my left and aim for between his legs. After a momentary split second I find him and he's already nice and hard. He moans as I rub him forcefully, feeling him grow larger against my touch.

Pulling away I drop to my knees. He's wearing a pair of black combat-style trousers which I soon have its belt unbuckled and the button and flies undone. I tug at his clothes and they fall easily down to his ankles to reveal his grey-coloured Calvin Klein's, bulging at the front under strain. I tear his pants down in an almost vicious manner, revealing his throbbing cock before me. I grab it with my right-hand and slowly wank him and its hot and as rigid as Hell. Caressing his balls with my left-hand I shuffle myself closer to him.

Without hesitation I open my mouth and swallow him, sensing his taste and size. He lets out a loud moan as I use my tongue along his length and over the tight sensitive skin of his frenum. I start to bob my head back and forth, running my teeth closer to his meat as I then take his full length to the back of my throat, almost gagging myself. Placing my right-hand at the base of his dick I pull it back hard in order to stretch his skin tighter over his shaft as I simultaneously start to lick and suck hard on his wood. I continue like this only for a short while as I don't want him to cum in my mouth or in my face, not yet anyway, as I want to save him for later.

Standing up I kiss him hard on the lips and try to guide him into the kitchen hand-in-hand. He stumbles and almost falls over as his clothes tangle around his feet making us both laugh.

Kicking off his work-boots and removing his trousers and pants we both hurry into the kitchen, it being the nearest and largest room next to the hallway.

By the sink unit we kiss again and I force my tongue into his mouth and he returns the favour. I take off his t-shirt to reveal his fully naked body before me, it being quite firm with nice muscles but a little on the overweight side. I kick off my trainers and undo my jeans as Carl runs his fingers between my legs and over the thin material on my knickers. I almost cum there and then as the sensation takes my breath away and makes my heart shudder. Removing them quickly I literally throw them off to one side of the kitchen, revealing my beautiful smooth pussy.

My t-shirt and bra are similarly discarded and we embrace and kiss again. The touch of his naked body against mine feels fantastic as we cling to each other and I can feel his hard cock against my swollen wet vulva as we bury ourselves in the moment.

I stand back from him and gently push him away with one-hand. He looks a little confused at my action at first but when I turn around and bend over the penny suddenly drops in his mind. Leaning over onto the white granite work-surface with my arms semi-crossed I stick my bum up into the air for him. In a moment I feel his cock kissing against my labia, gently at first and then with one slightly unexpected thrust I feel his length inside me. My mind rockets into outer-space and I feel my brain is about to explode as he begins to ram me from behind whilst holding my tight belly with his right-hand and my left-breast with his other, squeezing it firmly but not too hard.

After a short while of pumping away inside me he screams that he's about to cum. I manage to pull away and quickly spin myself around, dropping him out of my hole. I fall to my knees once again just in time for Carl to spit his load into my mouth, letting his spunk pool on my tongue until he's fully spent. He moans and groans as his muck dribbles from my open mouth out and down my chin and onto my tits. Using both my hands

I rub his mess all over them, especially around my proud sensitive nipples.

With his cock in one-hand I begin to wank him again as I try to extract every last drop of jism out of him. One small pearlescent drop trickles from his slit and falls to the smooth tiled kitchen floor. I bend down and lick it up.

I get to my feet and we both look at each other and laugh at what has just happened between us. Carl excuses himself to the bathroom to clean himself up whilst I stay in the kitchen to retrieve my clothes from the floor and to wipe up the mess. Using several sheets of kitchen towel I begin to wipe off Carl's spunk from my mouth and breasts as well as from the floor just as he re-enters the room.

We look at each other and laugh once again as he redresses. We small-talk about nothing in particular, just crap really. As he goes to leave we kiss again, just a small one on the lips with him now fully clothed and myself still naked and raw.

"I'll call you later about the car Sarah" he says standing in the open doorway, about to go and leave me all alone once again.

"Okay, I'll see you later" I say, peering around the edge of the front door so no-one can see my nakedness.

I close the door and laugh out loud to myself. How much did I need that? I jump in the shower to clean myself up and wash away both Carl's drying spunk and my own mess. I dry myself off and redress, changing my underwear in the process as my knickers are wet and smelly from my own juice.

***

I settle down in the living room with a nice cold bottle of San Miguel lager that soon cools me down nicely. I smile to myself once again at today's events as Lacey jumps up onto my lap and settles herself down and starts purring, poor old thing.

A little while later my phone rings and it's Carl, the car's all fixed and he asks me if I would like him to bring it back to my place? I decline his offer with lots of sweetness and all that crap, telling him that I'll come down and collect it myself. I don't want him to get the wrong idea, I do like him and I wanted to have sex with him earlier but that's as far as it's going to go between us and no more. This was a one-off and nothing else. We are all mercenaries to different degrees and with different wants and needs. I don't want to be his bit on the side. I want more freedom than that.

I stroll down the road without a care in the World to collect the car. Carl isn't in the front office when I arrive but I do spot him talking to another customer through the reception window that looks into the workshop. We exchange a small wave and a coy smile.

The bill for the repair comes to just over £60 which I pay on my Debit card. Apparently there was something wrong with one of the plugs, whatever that means? As long as its fixed I don't care, I've got my car back and I got screwed into the bargain - result!

4

Steve

For some time now I've been thinking about joining a dating agency but for some reason I've never actually had the courage to physically do it. Maybe it's because I find the whole idea a bit dodgy in meeting some total stranger in a pub somewhere as there are so many weirdo's around these days I just don't know what I might be letting myself in for?

Anyway, I've suddenly plucked up enough courage to at least have a look; there can't be any harm in that can there?

There are so many websites to choose from it's not true. Some seem okay on the face of it whilst others are definitely a no-no. The reviews from some of the girls who have experienced the dodgy ones are terrifying to say the least; I certainly don't want to get mixed up in any of that crap that's for sure.

After some 2-hours of looking and deliberating, I think and hope that at long last I've found a decent one. The vast majority of the reviews are good and the company is fully registered so I'm going to take the plunge. Like a lot of the sites I've looked at the joining fee is free but to actually contact and hook-up with someone you have to pay. In the case of the one I've chosen it's £29.99 for one-month subscription, which I personally think is a bit steep but I pay it anyway.

Obviously the site wants to know some personal details. I was going to expand the truth a little about my age and say that I'm 28 but why should I lie? Although I actually consider myself both ageless and timeless I type in my real age of 32. I fill out my online profile form which includes all the usual standard stuff like hair colour, eye colour, height, weight, ethnic origin and all that crap. Then there's some rather more personal questions such as my favourite sexual position and the like, I type in "doggy", and other such things. For anal I reply "yes", bisexual - "no", couples - "no" and so on etc etc.

A photo is also required so I post a really nice one of myself taken by an ex-boyfriend a few years ago of me lying on my back on the bed with my beautiful long legs pointing skywards. If that doesn't pull the guys then nothing will!

Just out of interest I've checked out some of the other girl's photos on this site, the competition that is, with the vast majority of those having just pictures of their breasts and vaginas but that really isn't my style at all. Don't get me wrong though, I'm after a guy to give me a good time and poke me hard but I don't want to attract some bloody psychopath! Also I'm not doing this looking for some sort of relationship or everlasting love or any of that shit either, despite the pressures of Mum, my sister, people at work or anyone else you might want to throw into the pot. All I'm looking for a nice guy to use as a fuck-buddy and maybe go out somewhere nice every now and then and that's it - no strings.

Men, they want all women to be a cross between a whore, a cook, a mother, a nurse and a cleaner, amongst other things. Well not me, I'm nobody's slave.

I use Lacey's name as my password, and with all my details approved by the website after a wait of about 5-minutes, I decide to have a good look around the site to see what's on offer.

The amount of Black and Asian guys on here is both unbelievable and a little disconcerting, so too is the number of Polish and other Eastern Europeans. I definitely do not want to get involved with any of them that's for sure; they don't have a fucking clue how to treat a girl, especially a white English one like me.

The total number of guys on here is absolutely amazing. According to my research beforehand, there are some 800 guys for every 200 girls just on this site alone! I never realized there were so many lonely people out there? I wonder how many of them are just like me? I find the statistics really sad. How did it all come to this?

Anyway, after making a note of a few fit guys - and not just the one's showing photos of their dicks! - I log off for the day. I'll have another look tomorrow.

***

It's a new day and I'm back online. I log on to the dating site and enter my password to view my profile. I can't believe that I've received 281 messages already, even though I only hooked up with them yesterday!

I take a closer look at those who've contacted me and some of these guys are unbelievable, old buggers that are old enough not only to be my father but my grandfather! They've got no fucking chance. I've also got no end of messages from Black, Asian and Eastern Europeans just as I expected; they've equally got no bloody hope in Hell of sneering me either. I delete the lot and block them from contacting me again, not even bothering to read their no doubt obviously disgusting and degrading messages. Bastards.

After filtering through the remaining messages I'm left with the grand total of thirteen guys who fit my want. Out of those I pick just three to send a return message back to. One of them, Steve, is a little older than me at 38 and is quite nice looking and has an amazingly fit body with fantastic abs. He has a gorgeous physique with nice defined muscles; he can screw me anytime he likes! I just hope and pray that he's as nice in the flesh as he is in his photo? That's assuming it is his real photo and he's not some 90-year old wanker?

I continue browsing at other guys just to pass the time - geeks, retards, fruit-loops, nerds, old farts, imbeciles, spotty teenagers, dick heads, junkies, ex-cons and creeps - the list is bloody never ending!

After some 45-minutes have elapsed I receive two messages back from a couple of the guys I Emailed earlier. One is from Steve, the guy with the fit body, with the other coming from Graham who's not quite as nice looking but I decide to read his message first.

I wish I hadn't. Its disgusting. He's obviously some sort of bloody mental case and has a problem with women, listing out all the horrible violent things he wants to do too me - smacking me around, fisting me and cutting-off all my hair. I'm not having any of that shit so I report him to the website and let them deal with him. What an evil bastard. I hope they're not all like him?

The other guy, Steve, thankfully, seems to be quite genuine and has sent me a lovely message, although by now I'm a little bit shaken by the first guy and very wary of taking things any further with anyone. He says he would like to meet up with me and asks me to message him back, which I do, in turn asking him to send me some more details about himself and when and where we can meet?

After several more messages back and forth between us I agree to meet up with him at the Bricklayers Arms pub in Ockley, just outside my home town at 7.30pm tomorrow night - yikes!

Bloody Hell! What have I done now? What have I bloody let myself in for this time? I really do hope and pray that Steve is a genuine guy and not some bloody psychopath? I message him back one last time to say "See you tomorrow night" and then log off. Oh my God!

***

Well, needless to say I didn't get much sleep last night, even though I had a couple of sleeping pills to knock myself out. The thought of what might and could happen with this guy tonight kept flying about in my mind, multiplying itself out of all proportion.

I must stop beating myself up. I guess there's no real reason to worry but I just don't know what could potentially happen? Apart from him poking me of course! Now I've got this far though I'm determined to see it through, although as ever I'll be on my guard, just in case.

After yet another continuously boring day at work - no surprise there then! - I'm back at home preparing myself for my date tonight with Steve. I've had a thorough scrub in the shower, dried myself off and added my full-on killer make-up, the total works this time as I'm not taking any prisoners tonight. The whole World had better be on standby as I know what I want and I'm going to get it!

As for my clothes, tonight I'm going to dress to the max also. I'm wearing a Royal-blue coloured sleeveless blouse from Miss Goody that I leave buttoned undone further down than is decent, showing off my cleavage. Although I'm a size-8 / 10, sometimes I have to get a size-12 just to fit everything in! Tonight though I've squeezed myself into a size-10 blouse just to accentuate my bust further, just to make damn sure everyone gets a good look at what I've got.

I'm also wearing a tight figure-hugging high-wasted pencil-cut skirt in cream that Mum custom-made for me. The waistband fits right up under my ribs to even further accentuate my bust. It also features 4-big buttons at the back to fasten and overall looks super-classy. I'm also going to wear those funky blue-suede Lola platform court shoes that I bought a while ago in Chichester, they're fantastic.

As for my underwear, I'm wearing a matching set of red lacy bra, knickers and suspender belt as I'm wearing stockings tonight, all from Ultimo. If that little lot doesn't get his pulse racing then he must be gay!

After a few squirts of *Mademoiselle* by Chanel I'm ready to rock. I look totally impeccable as well as gorgeous.

I arrive at the "Bricks" at 7pm, half an hour early, as I want to get a drink or two down my neck before Steve shows his face. That's assuming he actually turns up of course as over the years I've grown accustomed to disappointment in everything I've come into touch with.

The pub's actually not too crowded which is good, but I still feel like that there's a million eyes upon me as I strut my way up to the bar. The woman serving is a good 10-years older than me and is no-way as good looking. I say "Hello" to her and order myself a lager, a pint of course, not some girly drink or measure.

As she pulls my drink I quickly glance around the pub looking for Steve to see if he's beaten me in getting here but the answer is no. Once again, as ever, I notice guys (and most of the girls also!) looking me up and down, all of them tearing me apart with their mixture of wanting and jealousy. They can all look, I don't care, but they can't touch me tonight, none of them can, I'm reserved for one guy only. When he turns up that is!

The barmaid puts my drink on the counter, telling me: "That'll be £3.80 please love". Turning back to her I hand her a £5 note from out of my clutch-bag, a white faux-leather one from New Look. As she takes my money and goes to the till to get my change I can't help noticing her quickly scanning my chest, it bulging and straining against the tightness of my blouse. I have a momentary smirk to myself before I take a sip of lager. Another enemy destroyed.

I sit my bum down in one of the many snugs around the pub, this one being the only one completely empty. I have my usual watch of my fellow humans as they go about their lives, all chatting away laughing and joking and looking at me and my beautiful long legs.

By now it's 7.20pm and in walks Steve. I spot him straight away and he's even more gorgeous in the flesh than I had hoped and is way taller than I imagined for some reason? He spots me also and heads over in my direction and my heartbeat goes through the roof as he nears me, whilst my oestrogen levels have definitely moved up a notch or two! I think I'm having an eye-gasm!

We exchange "Hellos" and kiss each other's cheeks, followed by the usual standard banter - "Have you been waiting long?", "Would you like another drink?" and all that crap.

He goes and orders himself a drink, the same as my own, and returns and plonks himself down right next to me. In fact a bit too close for comfort actually considering that we've only just met but I let it slide.

We chat away for ages, hitting it off quite well. He tells me that he's only been on the dating site for a few days - so he says - and that I'm the first girl that he's actually met up with. I really don't know whether to believe him or not but I have to give him the benefit of the doubt I guess? There has to come a point where you have to trust someone but there is always something subconsciously nagging away in the back of my mind. And I'm not talking about my Mum either!

With our second-round of drinks almost finished the conversation turns to the main topic of our meeting - i.e. going back to my place. Once again my pulse quickens and I'm forced to breathe through my mouth to get enough air into my lungs. We decide to drink up and leave right now.

Heading for the car park I take the lead and I can sense him checking out my body (which is superb of course, need you ask?). Steve offers to drive and I readily accept, it's only a few miles back to my place and I don't mind leaving my car in the pub car park as it's quite safe and secure and has CCTV anyway. He opens the passenger-side door of his car for me - a silver VW Golf GTI - just like a gentleman should, and I slide-in bum first and then legs. Just like a woman should.

I'm so fucking nervous I am literally shaking, although I'm also as horny as Hell and I can't stop thinking about him being naked and touching me and loving me, running his big man-hands over my hot smooth skin! Oh bloody Hell! We drive off heading North on the A29 towards the direction of my home town and then onto the A24. I look across at him as he drives, just how I like a man to do it - fast and sure. As he changes into top gear I place my right-hand onto his left, catching him a little by surprise but he smiles at my action. When I let go he leans over to me and reaches out with his hand and touches my right-breast as we speed along!

He's a bit fucking cheeky isn't he?

Even so I love it and want more and harder and we both laugh. From my chest he relocates down to my right-thigh and tries to put his hand up between my legs but the tightness of my skirt prevents him getting any higher and so he leaves it there and squeezes me.

We arrive at my place in only 15-minutes. He switches off the engine and we lean towards each other and kiss quickly and gently. I really don't care (I do really) as I'm going to seize this moment and run with it. Exiting the car we hold hands like lovers as we enter my flat and kiss again once inside with the front door firmly shut, blocking out the prying eyes of the outside World.

I guide Steve into the living room which I've already pre-prepared in anticipation with cushions scattered all over the floor, sofa and chairs. On the coffee table are items from my special draw - condoms, some lubricant, a packet of wipes and other things. I fix us both some more drinks, another lager for him and a large neat vodka for the special girl, this being Vladivar, my preferred brand.

Steve sips his drink but I take down a large gulp of mine as some kind of pseudo-defence / stiffener as then we kiss again. I want him so badly that I feel a little bit sick. With the vodka giving me courage I immediately aim my hand between his legs where I find him already super-hard and he lets out a deep moan as I rub him. He puts his bottle down on the sideboard next to us and places one hand on my right-breast with the other running over my hole.

I almost cum there and then at the sensation of Steve's fingers on my vagina as we both throw ourselves into the fire. He releases me and with both hands rips open my blouse, its buttons pinging off all over the room, revealing my heaving breasts. Hey, I really liked that blouse!

In under 2-seconds he has my bra removed and alternately begins licking my nipples whilst squeezing my breasts hard. I feel myself becoming wetter as he sucks me as he then drops to his knees and starts pulling at my belly-rings with his teeth. He unbuttons my skirt at the rear and it crumples to the floor and then pushes one hand between my legs, making him wet.

Unclipping my stockings from its belt Steve pulls each one down and off along with my heals, closely followed by my knickers. I reveal to him my shinny smooth vulva which by now has engorged itself. He repositions me down onto the sofa and without hesitation I suddenly feel the beautiful sensation of his tongue lapping at my minge, darting over and between my lips and flicking at my clit. A shudder hits my body like ice, making my whole being shake and twitch as he purges me of self-control.

I don't know why it is but a guys tongue in my hole always seems to work better for me than his cock and I cum myself and scream out loud. I collapse into myself as I'm eaten and cum again from my new love.

Totally spent, Steve stands before me and quickly removes his clothes. As I watch him I am in complete awe of his presence - he's so fucking gorgeous, beautiful even - with a perfect fit body and a cock to die for. Not only must it be a good 8 to 9-iches in length but its really thick as well with an enormous wide knob.

I don't know what to do as I'm so knackered from my orgasms and the sight of this fantastic specimen of man that I just lay there on the sofa staring at him in shock. I needn't have worried as I don't have long to wait as Steve clambers onto the sofa next to me with his weapon level with my face.

He reaches out with his left-hand and forcefully inserts his thumb into my mouth and I start to suck it. His thumb is soon replaced by his index finger and I suck on that also. He then pushes 2-fingers into my mouth and I fall in love with him.

Removing them he moves in closer to me, the size of his knob making me question whether I'll be able to take him? I've never had one this size in all my days!

I slowly tongue at him, sensing the smooth velvety texture of his helmet and he moans and loves me back. I play with his balls with one hand and then use my tongue on them, taking one of his eggs into my mouth.

I return to his dick and run my lips around his knob, tasting his skank. I have fallen in love with it and swallow him, trying hard to keep my tongue under his shaft but it's not easy as I take him into my mouth as far as I dare.

Steve moans in ecstasy and jerks his hips as he fucks my mouth slowly. I tug on his balls and taste his pre-ejaculate as he again sighs loudly and then shouts at me that he's about to cum already. I eject him just as he shoots his potent gloopy load into my face, into my eyes, over my hair, up my nose and over and into my mouth. He screams in relief of his ejaculation as I laugh at the soaking of his mess.

Reaching for the packet of wipes I try to remove Steve's cum the best I can, it's fucking everywhere! His wood has also faded a little so I wank him and he re-pressurises sure enough. I reposition myself on all fours to let him fuck me from behind, my favourite. Now fully-hard once again I rubber him and turn back around for him to fuck me doggy-style. His meaty cock feels so fucking good as it slides into my vagina and I enter the gates of Heaven itself as he bangs away at me. The sheer size of him throbbing inside my body drives me insane and I order him to go harder and I implode, making me buck like a wild animal.

We continue for an age until I demand something more, I want him to fuck me anally. He wants to also but also has a demand, to tie me up first.

Now I'm not really into bondage *per se* but I agree anyway, in fact he can do whatever he fucking likes to me as that's the mood I'm in! He removes his leather belt from his discarded jeans and binds my wrists together tightly behind my back. On my knees I reposition myself on the floor with my face kissing the carpet and my bum stuck up in the air for all the World to see. What a beautiful picture I must be?

Steve squirts some lube into my bum-crack and fingers it into my hole. It feels cold and somehow sharp as he uses one finger gently inside me and I want him now. Now does become now as I feel his hard cock touching my ring, the coolness of the lube making me shake like mad. I feel a little pain as he pushes his thick cock into me making me cry "ow ow ow". I breathe my very last breath as he fully enters my bum and I die and I'm resurrected at one and the same moment.

He fucks me slowly but hard and I almost pass-out at the sensation, it's almost too much pressure. After several minutes of fucking he's about to cum once again and pulls out of me, ripping off his rubber and firing his spunk over my back and my bound arms, over my beautiful blonde hair and my bum cheeks which are now red and raw from its beating even though it feels so good.

Steve unties my wrists and we both collapse to the floor in exhaustion and laughter. I really fucking needed that! Surprisingly I regain my breath quicker than expected and continue playing with his cock and balls again with one hand. Semi-erect I suck him and lick at him and then straddle him in a 69.

I don't usually like sucking a guy's cock this way around as I can never seem to get my tongue under the clevis of his knob properly. But with this one I just don't care, I'm totally in love with Steve's dick and I want it in my mouth forever.

As I suck on him he laps away at my vagina, swirling his tongue around inside my hole and over my clitoris. Believe me, to say that by this time that I'm totally knackered would be an understatement to say the least! Steve probably feels pretty much the same I would guess but we continue to eat each other slowly.

Out of the corner of my cum-smeared eye I catch a glimpse of Lacey, sitting there staring at me like some sort of Egyptian sculpture with her big round yellow eyes. I wonder what's she's thinking? She's intelligent enough to work out what I'm doing; it's not the first time that she's seen me fucking some guy that's for sure.

I cum again in under a minute and spit over Steve's mouth and he drinks me. It takes me a bit longer to milk the bull but sure enough I have him. This time though I want him totally, letting him ejaculate his muck to the back of my throat. I swallow some and spit the rest back out onto his knob and down his cock as I head him with my mouth and tongue.

My head fills with the taste of lager, vodka, cock, balls, spunk and man and I overdose on the effect of each and every one of them. I am the happiest girl on Planet Earth. I love being me and I love it and cum as I suck him.

We are both completely fucked as our sex-meet comes to its inevitable end, laying there next to each other naked on the floor holding hands, both of us staring at the ceiling in total exhaustion. We chat some small-talk and other crap and it's lovely and everything is beautiful in the World.

We shower together to wash away our love and the hot water is wonderful on our skin and we embrace and kiss and touch. I dry Steve's body and he's beautiful. He then dries me off and I'm beautiful also.

In the living room we kiss and drink tea. Steve runs the back of his fingers over my naked body and plays with one of my nipples. I giggle and moan like a girl and touch his cock and balls with one-hand. We've both had a great time and promise to meet each other again, a promise that is bound to be broken I'm sure just as they all are. I watch him dress as I sit there naked with my mug of sweet tea.

He has to go and we both head towards the front door. I don't want him to stay tonight anyway as I want and need my own space. But even so at the same time I want him to stay with me forever; I want him to fuck me forever, to love me forever but none of it will happen.

We kiss once more and he touches me between my legs and I die. I throw my arms around his neck and I wish we could meld into just one person, a single human being so we can love and fuck ourselves forever and nothing else.

He leaves me and I stand there naked in the doorway. I don't need clothes for anything. Not now. Not this day. He waves me "Goodbye" and I blow a kiss too him. I watch him drive away as he leaves me alone once again all by myself.

I shut and lock the door to the rest of the World as it doesn't exist to me. I pour myself a large glass of white from the fridge and feed Lacey as she curls herself around my ankles in anticipation of filling her belly. Her fur feels lovely and soft against my skin and I touch my vagina.

I smile to myself for being me and the power I control over my life and the rest of mankind.

***

It's the day after Steve and I'm sitting here at work typing shit into my computer like a moron. I'm trying hard not to think about him too much but it's difficult to block him out of my mind, men are my pleasure, as are other things.

I click away on the keyboard inputting data from customer's orders as this is my job. This is the other side of my life, the side that I hate and resent right down to the very core of my existence.

I am rich beyond my means but I have no money. I am in the gutter but I'm also a Queen.

5

Tattoo

It's Saturday and I've got an appointment this morning at 9.30am with John, my ace tattoo artist at his tattoo and piercing studio in the next town.

I'm having some cover-up work done on my right shoulder of a tattoo that I had done years ago by some other artist, that being of the ex-boyfriends name, the one that I can't even bare to mention. I've got an idea for a portrait of my cat Lacey to cover up the old tattoo but I'm not sure it's going to be possible to fix it that easily.

John himself is a lovely guy but way too old for me though as he must be in his fifties - and married with 3-kids! I'm pretty certain he wants to screw me even so, the same as any red-blooded male does.

Because of potential leaking of blood and ink from the new tattoo I'm wearing a black blouse this morning from Ivanna so hopefully it won't show if it does decide to leak, which it probably will, they always do. In contrast with the blouse I'm wearing a white mini pencil-skirt from INTU, and a pair of white 1940's-style MaryJane strap-shoes from Babygirlboutique which I adore. Underneath I'm wearing a matching red lacy bra and knickers with suspenders from Ultimo which in total makes me look and feel really hot. I've also gone for a bit of a vampish look to my makeup today to accentuate my sharp cheekbones, whilst my perfume is *Luxe* by Avon.

I arrive at John's studio early as the parking on this road is a total bitch. Sure enough, when I get here there are no spaces to be had so I'm forced to go around the block in circles in the hope that someone moves their car and I can sneak in. Amazingly my luck seems to be with me as a space opens up after three tours of the block. Parking is so tight around here because of the train station opposite the studio, even on a Saturday, as the station has no car park itself. The number of flats squashed onto this road doesn't help either.

I enter the studio to find John sitting behind his reception desk opening his mail.

"Hi Sarah, how the Devil are you?" he says in his ever cheerful manner.

"I'm great thanks, how are you?"

"Can't complain, you know?"

"Been busy then have you?" I say.

"Yeah, fairly busy. The piercing side of things has really taken off."

John has previously pierced my belly-button three times and my ears on so many occasions I can't remember. He also put rings through my nipples a few years ago but they didn't "take" and migrated out, much to my annoyance and pain. Fortunately they're okay now and are both fully healed.

As John opens his last envelope I wander around the studio looking at all the "Flash" on the walls. He's already prepared the stencil for my tattoo as I Emailed it to him several weeks ago so everything is pre-set in advance and ready to go.

Free at last, John calls me into his back room and my heartbeat quickens as it's time to go under the needle. Going to a tattoo artist for me is a bit like going to see my Doctor; I don't mind stripping-off in front of him as it's not a sexual experience, it's purely professional and for me I find it quite spiritual.

John shows me a few modifications that he's made to my drawing, nothing much, just a few small simple changes. I agree with his mods but with a couple of minor adjustments of my own just to get it how I want. I remove my blouse and place it over the back of a spare chair in the studio. John looks at me briefly, checking out my body, and then continues with the setting-up of the ink into little red plastic cups in their special stainless-steel holder.

I sit down sideways on what was once a dentist's chair and pull down my bra-strap over my right-arm, giving John a clear area to work on. He squirts my shoulder with some foul-smelling antiseptic spray which gets right up my nose and immediately makes me sneeze and him laugh! Next he applies the stencil of my drawing over the top of the old tattoo to be covered up. I agree with the placement in the mirror and off we go, with John switching the tattoo machine into life and it buzzes-away like a bee trapped in a tin can.

Nothing can prepare you for the first stab of the needle into your skin as John begins the outline. It feels like that he's actually cutting me with a knife as the outline is done with a thinner needle than the shading one which hurts not so nearly as bad. After only half-an-hour of buzzing-away the outline is finished and it's time for the shading.

After a quick wipe-clean of the blood and excess ink, John cheekily throws me a line:

"So, how's your love life then Sarah?"

"Oh, there's no-one special but I've had my moments!" I quip back.

"Yeah, I bet you have" he comes back.

"Now now, that's enough of that, remember you're married."

He laughs at my defensive reply but then you know what men are like, any hole's a goal with them.

With that it's straight on with the colouring-in of the outline. As I've already told you, the shading-in is not nearly as painful, in fact after a while it becomes quite therapeutic and somewhat soothing and I actually begin to feel a little bit sleepy. Some 40-minutes later it's all over and my fresh new piece of art is complete and to my relief the ex's name has disappeared forever, joy! John wipes my shoulder clean and then tapes some kitchen paper over the raw tattoo. I gently pull up my bra-strap and it stings me as I place it over my make-shift bandage.

I sit on the edge of the chair for a minute or two to try and get my bearings as I still feel a bit light-headed. Slowly standing up I put my blouse back on as John cleans and clears his tattoo equipment and we chit-chat about stuff.

We make our way back into the reception area and its still deserted as John is only doing pre-booked appointments today and the next customer / victim hasn't turned up yet. I count out the agreed price of £120 in cash from my purse, a black Hobo one from Purple Leopard, and hand it over with loads of "Thanks" and other pleasantries from both sides. I move towards him, giving him a small hug and an air-kiss to his cheek with another "Thank you" as I then make my exit and leave.

You would not believe how much of a relief it is to get that cover-up done so successfully, wiping away a nasty stain from my life that has long since ended and erased from my memory.

***

I make my way home with my shoulder stinging me a little. The amount of bloody traffic is atrocious and it takes me almost three-quarters-of-an-hour to just eleven-miles!

Back home in my bathroom I remove my blouse and bra and gaze at the patch on my shoulder in the reflection in the mirror. It has also leaked a little blood - I told you it would! - so I'm extra careful in removing it and it sticks momentarily. The cover-up seems pretty good with no sign of "What's-his-face's" name anywhere to be seen. I really hope it stays that way to.

After gently washing it in warm water I pat it semi-dry with a few sheets of loo paper. I move around in the mirror to take-in the full view of my new tat and it looks so cool that it starts to make me feel really horny. I decide to have a little drink and a little play as the effects of this morning's blood-loss from the tattoo has turned me onto myself.

I strip-off completely and head into the living room, pouring myself a large vodka, neat of course. It's not long before a heady warming glow begins to filter throughout my naked body and I feel so alive, like I've just been reborn. With my glass in my left-hand I move my other down to between my legs. I feel a sudden sting from my new tattoo as I start to jerk myself gently. I dip the fingers of my right-hand into my vodka and rub my clit with it, making my oyster glisten and hot as it stings me a little and I love it, the added wetness making me want to fuck with myself.

I down the last remains of my drink, put my empty glass down and make my way into the bedroom where the bottom draw of my bedside cabinet contains my special toys. I select my purple Doc Johnson multi-speed vibrator and squat down next to my bed and fuck my mouth with it, making myself cough in the process.

I move onto the bed itself and bending over on my knees I insert the vibro into my wanting vagina. It buzzes away as I slowly move it in and out of my hole, making me groan with its hardness. I pull it out and grab my tube of lubrication from the draw, squeezing some of it onto the wet shaft. Back in the same position I slowly push my plastic cock into my bum-hole, making it sting as it slides its way in buzzing away. The sensation makes my legs turn to jelly but I love it and push it in further, making me jerk spasmodically.

I get up and walk back to living room with the device still up my bum, holding it there with one-hand as I slug down more vodka straight from the bottle with the other. I am totally out of my mind from the effects of the tattoo, the smell, the noise, the blood, the image, John, the vodka, the vibrator, being alive, being me, being a woman, being free, being gorgeous, having tits, my car, Lacey, my flat, my teeth, my legs, my fingers, my eyes, my cunt, my life, my death, my independence, my imagination, skin, dirt, hair, cock, my hands, my toes, my heart, my spine, my bike, my health, fucking, shit, wanking, money, TV, music, sucking, cum, sucking cum, food, air, fire, shopping, my past, my future, my country, planet Earth, the Sun.

All these subjects fly through my mind in a matter of seconds.

***

I wake up to find myself on the floor in total darkness. I feel like shit, like someone has shot me right between my eyes. I start hyperventilating as I try to come to terms with my situation. I must regain control or I will implode.

I roll over and feel something cold and wet underneath my naked body. As I reach under myself I realise that its my vibrator that has fallen out of my rear-end and is laying there dead, its batteries spent. I throw it to one side and try to stand up but it's no good, I am totally knackered and so I have to crawl into the kitchen. I just about manage to flick the light switch on but the glare is so intense that it burns my eyes and I have to cover them immediately with both hands.

As I gradually get used to the light I begin to visualise the time on the kitchen clock. It says 3.20. That can't be right? How come it's so bloody dark outside at this time of the afternoon? It soon dawns on the thick bitch that I am that it now is of course the following morning and that I've been unconscious for about fifteen-hours!

My thoughts then switches to Lacey. Where the Hell is she? I eventually stumble to my feet and find her fast asleep on my bed, seemingly without a care in the World - typical! I leave her alone and head back into the living room, shut the blinds and turn the lights on to survey the damage.

The half a bottle of vodka I downed lays empty on the floor next to my vibrator which is bloody and soiled, as is the carpet, not only from my bum but from the tattoo as well. Obviously that has leaked some ink onto the floor where I collapsed.

The coffee table is now upside-down with its glass top cracked. The hand-made fruit bowl that was on top of the table, the bowl being the one I bought years ago in the Lake District and is (was) one of my treasures, is smashed to pieces.

I drop to my knees and burst into tears. Why does this shit always happen to me?

I suddenly feel something brush up against my skin. It's Lacey, woken to the noise of my tears. She hates me crying and wails at me which in turn makes me cry even more so I pick her up and cuddle her and we both weep together.

I decide to leave the mess on the floor until tomorrow - or should that be today? - as I can't be arsed to do it now. I throw a couple of bed-sheets over the lot just in case Lacey goes near it and cuts herself on the broken glass.

I really must sort myself out as I feel a right fucking state. I hit the shower, catching a glimpse of myself in the bathroom mirror as I pass. A look of sheer terror sweeps over me as I come face to face with my own self - what a fucking mess!

Stupid bloody cow.

I suppose it's a good thing that it's the weekend as I would have been completely bollocksed if this shit had happened mid-week. The real horror of what might have happened suddenly sweeps over me - what if I hadn't woken up at all? I could have bloody killed myself in a drunken stupor?

What a stupid bloody thing to do.

What a fucking waste.

I will never drink again.

6

Leaving Party

A few weeks ago - four to be exact - Richard, the company post-boy and "Chest Admirer", handed-in his resignation notice. Apparently he's leaving to go and work for his father in the building trade or something like that? Anyway, he's invited everyone at work to his leaving do tonight at the White Horse pub in town at 7.30pm. Richard's a nice guy really and I will miss him, even though he does keep looking at my bangers!

I guess I'll go along to say "Goodbye" and "Good luck". It's also a good excuse to dress-up and have a drink or two or three, and as the pub is within easy walking distance from my flat there's no need to take the car, another good excuse for more drinking!

I've microwaved an expensive ready-meal that I bought from a farm shop out of town a couple of days ago, and that's what I've just finished eating. It'll give me a bit more time to get ready for tonight's little party at the pub instead of wasting precious time cooking a proper meal.

All finished up, I wash my dinner down with a large vodka as it's time to get ready. Tonight I'm going to wear a white sheer-cotton blouse from Lyst, open down low of course, with a white cotton pencil-cut skirt from Alibaba that has a large split up the back so everyone can see my legs to the full. I'm also going bare-legged. On my feet I'm putting on my pair of blue platform heals which I've nick-named my "Chichester" shoes. As for my underwear I'm going to wear my black lacy Ann Summers set as it shows right through my clothes, something that I'm doing on purpose just so everyone can see my beautiful figure. I already know that the whole ensemble will all work well together and that I'll be the star female attraction of the evening.

With my full killer make-up on and smelling like a princess - my perfume tonight is *Poison* by Christian Dior - I kiss Lacey *au revoir* and head off into town.

I can't believe the High Street has deserted so quickly after the rush hour; it's almost like a bloody ghost-town except for a few cars here and there. A large white van drives past me going in the opposite direction, with the three guys sitting in the front - typical builder types - all staring at me. The driver sounds his horn and all three of them shout at me through the driver's open window, it being a very warm and muggy evening, coming out with comments like:

"Allo darlin"

"Where you going gorgeous?"

"Fancy a shag"

"Show us yer tits"

I stick 2-fingers up at them and walk on, although the image of all three of them banging the living-daylights out of me at the same time quickly flashes across my mind for a couple of seconds. Fucking arseholes.

A bit further up the road a group of about ten or so youngsters, all in their late-teens I guess, girls as well as boys, have gathered outside the local kebab shop in the High Street. They're all standing around drinking cans of lager, smoking, swearing and dropping bits of disgusting kebab on the pavement and being a general pain in the arse. I walk straight through the middle of them, looking straight ahead.

They all stop and stare at me like I'm some sort of Queen riding along on horseback at a parade. Not one of them says a single solitary word too me as I pass by but I know exactly what they're all thinking. The guy's can't believe their eyes at the vision of my loveliness whilst the girls look at me in ultimate envy, they want to kill me and rip me apart such is their jealousy.

I reach the White Horse unscathed, both physically and mentally, as nothing and no-one can touch me, not this day. I am above everyone I've seen today and will be again tomorrow. Inside the pub its rammed full of people, mainly well-wishers for Richard, who I spot propped-up at the bar obviously totally pissed out of his head already and it's only just gone 7.30pm! Standing next to him and desperately trying to hold him up is some gawky little girl wearing far too much make-up and with the body of a 12-year old and who I later find out is his girlfriend!

Well, he kept that one quiet didn't he? All this time he was looking me up and down and fantasizing about my breasts and he already has a girl!

From out of nowhere, Inga, my supervisor, sidles up to me and asks me what I'd like to drink?

"Oh, a lager please" I say, somewhat surprised by her unexpected offer.

"A pint though" I shout after her as she turns and wanders over to the bar.

Rachael then appears and comes and stands by me and we chat about our day and take the piss out of our fellow workers and other people in the pub. It seems like I'm the last person from the company to arrive which makes me feel somehow uneasy? Despite being quite a few pounds overweight - maybe even a couple of stone? - Rachael still looks really nice in her blue jeans and dark-grey blouse. She's also done her make-up really well but its still nowhere as perfect as mine as I have the better face and bone-structure.

Inga returns and hands me my drink and swans off to leave us to take the piss out of her also. Time passes quickly as do the drinks. We order a couple more at the bar where there are four guys standing around all bunched together - not from our party - who immediately begin to eye Rachael and myself up and down. One of them, a real mouthy-type with presumably a small dick, comes and starts sniffing around us like a dog on heat. He starts to chat the both of us up and offers to buy us more drinks and to come and join him and his mates. Rachael - impressively quickly I have to say! - turns to him and declines his offer and then adds that both she and I are "partners".

"What do mean partners?" he enquires.

"She means that we're together" I snap back at him, putting him back in his box.

As I say this I put my arm around Rachael's shoulder and pull her close to me, with her doing the same as well as planting a light kiss to my left- cheek. Mr. Small-Willy stands there totally lost and dumbfounded so we grab our drinks, tell him to "Fuck off" and head over to the other side of the bar laughing, leaving him standing there alone and dejected like the wanker he is.

Rachael has to go for a pee and so makes her excuses and departs for the loo, leaving me standing at the bar on my own even though I'm surrounded by a hundred people - as per bloody usual.

There's a couple of guys staring at me from the other side of the bar, both obviously younger than me and both obviously talking about me judging by their manner. Before I even have time to mouth at them to "Piss off" they both wander over to me and introduce themselves. The one with all the chat - Alan - is actually quite sweet whilst the other, I didn't catch his name due to all the bloody noise in the pub, is okay but not nearly as nice looking.

After a brief exchange of mindless chat I suddenly become so bored out of my skull at their banter that I just walk away, although not before Alan gives me his name, phone number and Email address on one of his business cards and asks me to "Give him me call sometime." I smile and tell him that I'll think about it as I make my escape. Tossers.

I know I'm still young (ish!) and still attractive with a killer figure and all that and guys look at me all the time, but I do wish sometimes that they would just leave me alone. I wish sometimes that I was invisible to them and escape their glare. Do you understand what I mean?

I smooch back over to the other side of the bar once again, back to where the four creeps were earlier, but thankfully they're nowhere to be seen. As is Rachael, who I appear to have lost contact with along the way somewhere? I stop and chat small-talk to some people from work, some that I've seen before and others that I've no-idea who the Hell they are. It makes no difference anyway as I'm even more bored now that I was before. I'm also a little bit pissed as I'm on my fifth drink of the evening, and that's not including the ones I had at home. I really mustn't mix my lager with vodka.

I check my watch and it's almost 9pm already and I really need to sit down as my feet are killing me - bloody shoes! I find myself heading towards young Jennifer, the office odd-ball, sitting there on her own as per usual, sipping on her glass of Coke - strictly no alcohol for her!

I say "Hi" and she smiles back at me a big beaming smile, unusual for her as she's normally got a gloomy face on her like the Angel of Death. I sit myself down next to her and desperately try to engage her in some sort-of conversation, which once again she surprisingly responds. She starts telling me that she didn't quite know what to wear for tonight as she doesn't get invited to many do's. No, really! I then notice that for once she's not dressed all in black like she usually is, although she does have a pair of black trousers on, and a pretty stylish black and white patterned blouse.

Sitting so close to her I can't believe how incredibly plain-looking she is, but then again I suppose she does have a certain amount of attractiveness about her, for the right guy of course? Or should that be the right girl? I ask her if she's seeing anyone at the moment and straight away she says a very firm "No" back to me. Talk about conversation killer! To extract myself from the ensuing deafening silence I tell her that "I'm just going for a quick pee." I really do have to go as lager tends to go right through me and I've already sunk quite a few by now.

In the toilet I sit there on the loo thinking about leaving the party and heading off home, I'm so fucking bored out of my skull that I can't explain. I tidy myself up and redress and start running my hands over my upper-body in a vain attempt to thrill myself out of my stupor. It's only a partial success - I'm still bored.

The next moment I hear someone come into the toilet and presumably wash their hands as I hear the sound of running water followed by stony silence. As I'm all done myself I flush the loo and open the cubicle door and to my surprise I find young Jennifer standing there drying her hands under the heat of the automatic hand-dryer. A little shocked to see her I just smile at her and she returns the same.

I wash my hands and dry them as she stands by the toilet door watching me, making me feel a little uncomfortable. As I go to leave she suddenly places one hand on my shoulder in a soft and gentle manner.

What the fuck is going on here?

To say that I'm a bit surprised would be an understatement! I just stand there frozen to the spot with my eyes and mouth open as Jennifer moves her hand over my shoulder and down towards my right-breast. Fucking Hell! I just cannot believe this is happening! Is this for fucking real or what? I feel like that I've suddenly turned to stone, I can't move my body in defence or anything.

My heartbeat begins to pick up pace as Jennifer's slim fingers move ever nearer to one of my breasts but I'm still unable to speak or move. I let out a small sigh as she touches me; circling my nipple with the back of her fingers and making it stand proud. She steps closer to me and kisses me gently on the lips and it's so soft and I love it, even though I don't want to. I then sense her other hand around my waist and automatically I embrace her, bringing her closer to my body and we squeeze ourselves together.

My mind goes from complete blank to spinning confusion. I don't even think of her as another woman or even a guy, to me right now she's just another human being that I'm kissing, touching and caressing.

At that precise moment the main toilet door opens and in walks three girls - none of whom are from our party thankfully - two of them giggling at us whilst the third just stares in horror. Jennifer and I collect ourselves together and exit the toilet, not saying a single word to them or each other.

As if on automatic pilot we abandon our drinks, the rest of our group and the party and leave the pub together, heading out into the car park. Once outside in the open air she reaches out her hand to grab my mine and I take it, all in complete silence. There is no need for words, what is there to say?

As we walk I notice her nice figure, tall and slim, almost willowy really. She walks along like a young woman should, proud and arrow-straight and with a lovely little wiggle to her small but perfect bum. I think I'm actually a little bit jealous!

She guides me over to her car, a silver Mazda saloon, and we both get in, still with neither of us say anything. I really don't know what the Hell I'm doing (I do really), it's like I'm on some kind-of preordained mission of discovery or something? I'm actually shaking like crazy!

"Do you live far from here?" she asks me in her soft, sweet voice.

"No, not really, it's only about half a mile away. We could go back to mine if you want?" I reply. What the fuck?

"Okay, I'd like that" she agrees without hesitation.

What the Hell am I thinking?

In fact, what the Hell am I saying?

The stillness in the car on the way to my place is a bit creepy to say the least but I really don't care. What has come over me? Has she put me under some kind of spell? All I can think of is the both of us naked together, two naked women enjoying each other's bodies. How crazy does that sound?

***

At my flat we walk inside hand-in-hand and with the front door firmly shut behind us we kiss again. It's electrifying; she is so soft that it's driving me insane! I feel her hand move towards my left-breast, squeezing me firmly, and then moving down to between my legs, running her fingers over my slit. Oh fucking Hell! I stick my tongue into her mouth and she does the same to me as I then guide her into my bedroom.

We collapse onto my bed as one, making us both laugh together, actually the very first time that I've ever heard her do so in all the years we've worked together.

I lay on my side on the bed looking at her as she squats down in front of me. In a moment she removes her blouse to reveal her body too me and her firm young breasts. With both hands behind her she removes her black push-up bra to expose her naked peaches. They're beautiful, way smaller than mine of course but very pert and with lovely upturned stiff nipples. I lean forward and suck on her left one, playing with it with the tip of my tongue. She giggles like a little girl as I suck her as then she removes her shoes and trousers to reveal her black knickers.

Acting on pure instinct I push my right-hand between her crotch and feel her wetness. She falls backwards on the bed and opens her legs too me and I touch her again, making her laugh and moan. I pull hard at her knickers and off they come, revealing her smooth shaved pussy, all shinny and wet.

In this crazy situation I now find myself in, I don't even think twice to myself as I go down on Jennifer's tight little vagina, firstly licking her labia and then poking my tongue deeply into her hole. I find her clit and flick my tongue over its velvety softness, sensing the taste and aroma of another woman in my mouth. It doesn't stop me as I bury my face into her; in fact I want more and more of her in my mouth as I eat her out.

She lays there screaming in total pleasure as then she cums onto my tongue, her oily goo discharging over me as I lick her fanny. I come up for air and let Jennifer catch her breath. As I start to remove all my clothes just the way she did, she lays there staring at me with awe in her eyes. With both of us now completely naked we smile a knowing smile at each other. I beckon her to get off the bed and we stand before each other and embrace and kiss passionately, the thrilling clash between two naked females.

Her body is so soft to touch and her smooth skin excites me beyond reality, making me dribble my juice down between my legs. The emotion blows my mind. Can I really be doing this with another girl? Should I be doing this with another girl? I really don't know the answer to either.

I touch one of her firm young breasts and she moans in my mouth. I feel one of her hands move down my back to my bum and she squeezes it hard and then around to the smooth mound above my box. I yell in ecstasy as she inserts 2-fingers into my vagina, making me squelch my fluid out onto her hand. She starts to wank me harder and harder as I tighten my grip on her slim body and in seconds she makes me cum in a mad orgasmic rhythm and I scream.

She pushes me gently back onto the bed with both my legs dangling over the edge with my feet not quite reaching the floor. Forcefully she spreads my legs apart and drops herself down onto her knees. Keeping her hands firmly on my inner thighs she starts to kiss my box, just as hard as she did my mouth. The sensation is incredible, she is way better than any guy I've had licking me. My brain instinctively wants me to close my legs as a natural reaction to her touch but still she continues to force them open as she starts sucking on my clit. I can't take any more and I explode my cum into her mouth and she drinks my liquid.

She says my cum "Tastes like honey" and orders me to get onto all fours as she climbs on to the bed behind me. I feel her place both her hands on my bum-cheeks and grabs them hard, pulling them apart to expose my hole. I jerk spasmodically as I feel her spit on me a mixture of her saliva and my own cum as then she pushes home the index-finger of her right-hand into me, wanking me slowly.

I feel like I'm on fire as one finger becomes two as then she starts to flick her tongue around my crevice. Removing both her fingers she then reinserts them back into my minge and wanks me rhythmically. She starts to lick at my bum-hole and I scream with delight and my mind goes numb, the effect is amazing as she plays with my vagina and anal passage and I want more - I want everything and now. Oh my God!

"Do you have any lube Sarah?" she asks me in her quiet little voice.

I grab a tube from my special toy draw and reposition myself back in the same place as she then squirts a load of it onto my bum-hole and the fingers of her right-hand.

"Just relax your whole body Sarah, this will be really beautiful. You're really going to enjoy what I'm going to do to you" she whispers.

I obey without question as I then feel her small fist push against my rectum. It's so fucking tight but without hesitation she forces her tiny hand inside me. The pain is almost too much to bear as she enters me and I feel like I'm about to pass out and that my pelvis is about to crack. In no time she has her whole hand right inside me and I scream in a mixture of terror and pure pleasure as she begins to move it around inside my passage. I start to feel a little sick but I just about manage to keep myself together, the pain is both excruciating and exciting and I love it as I love her.

After several minutes of fucking me she removes her hand with a funny squelchy plopping sound and we both laugh as she begs me to do the same to her. I try to regain some composure to myself but it's not easy, I'm shaking all over and my body has turned to ice. It takes me at least a couple of minutes to calm myself down.

Jennifer repositions herself with her head on one of my soft pillows and her pert little bum stuck up in the air - she's obviously done this before! Adding plenty of lube to my right-hand and her bum, I push a couple of my fingers into her sweet little puckered hole. She cries in pleasure and pain as I wank her, slowly at first and then way harder. I then manage to get all four of my fingers into her, making her scream louder. Then, curling my thumb under my hand I manage to push my whole hand into her in one fatal shove and she loves me and cries.

I find the whole fisting thing a little disgusting but I'm caught up in the moment of my lesbian adventure with Jennifer. Anyway, I don't really care as I'm too busy enjoying my first girl-on-girl experience and I'll go along with anything she wants of me.

After fist-fucking her we hold each other tightly and kiss; it is so beautiful that my heart melts away.

We both make our way to the bathroom hand-in-hand to shower together and wash away our love. The hot water splashes down on her young naked skin and looks so good as it runs down her face onto her pert breasts, making them glisten. We both run our hands over each other's soapy bodies and it makes me feel so alive to touch another naked woman that I wonder to myself why I haven't tried this before? I just cannot believe how sensual she is compared to a guy.

There isn't really much to report after all that. The evening ended with me helping Jennifer to get dressed followed by some small-talk and another drink - a large neat vodka for me and yet another Coke for her. I remain naked as we hold each other and we kiss one last kiss with passion and more touching of breasts and vaginas and then she is gone into the night.

I must say that I didn't sleep much that night, my mind being in complete turmoil at what I had done. None of this was helped of course by me drinking way too much alcohol yet again, not to mention the throbbing pain in my rear-end! At least the slight bleeding seems to have subsided for now. I was really dreading it haemorrhaging all over the place; that would have really ruined my beautiful night with my little Jennifer.

***

The following morning back in the office both Jennifer and I smile and say "Hello" and exchange other pleasantries but that is the extent of our communication for the whole day. Our secret little lesbian adventure is never mentioned ever again. We live in a strange World don't we?

In hindsight I have no regrets about having a sexual encounter with another woman. I suppose it's all part of life's adventure and if I ever found myself in a similar situation then I guess that I'd probably do it again.

That doesn't make me gay to my mind, maybe it makes me bisexual, I don't know? To me personally I believe it makes me individual, independent and free, and if people can't understand that then that's their tough shit.

7

Kate

I received a text message last night at 11.21pm from my sister Kate, although it's only now, at 10.05am the following morning - Saturday - that I actually read the bomb-shell words before me. She's 3-months pregnant with her first child - my niece or nephew. I'm going to be an auntie!

I can't believe what I'm reading as I lay here in bed; the message doesn't seem to sink into my brain and just hovers above my head like a mysterious cloud. I suddenly feel much older, like I'm in my forties or fifties, more like a grandmother than an impending aunt and it scares me.

I kind-of feel sorry for my younger sister even though we've never really been that close. She's nowhere near as strong as I am mentally and I wonder how she's going to cope with having a kid in tow? We also have a completely different outlook on life. How could she have let this happen, especially with that dick-head boyfriend of hers? How irresponsible can you get?

All of a sudden my mobile rings, making me jump out of my skin and almost frightening me to death - it's Mum.

"Hi Mum" I say wearily.

"Oh Sarah, have you heard the wonderful news? Kate's going to have a baby, isn't it amazing? Are you up?" she bleats.

"Yes I'm up (sort of) and yes I've heard" I counter sarcastically as I just know what's coming in my direction next.

"I always thought you would be the first one to give me a Grandchild?" she whines.

I WANT

"Yes well, I'm not interested in having kids as I keep saying" I fire back at her at a hundred-miles-an-hour as by now I'm totally pissed-off by this never-ending line of attack. Why does it always end up at this same ridiculous point every bloody time we speak?

I end our conversation by telling Mum that there's someone at the front door and I have to go, even though I know that she doesn't believe a single word I say anyway.

I lay here thinking about the coming months and years at the situation my sister has got herself into, the same for the poor kid as well. The nappies, the crying, my sister losing control, the thick boyfriend disappearing off the face of the Planet, no money, the sick, the smell, the sleepless nights and Mum running around like a headless chicken as she fruitlessly tries to take control. The predictable list of this future scenario goes on and on. It's a fucking nightmare.

I somehow feel like I'm missing out on something? I feel that something is missing from my life but I don't know what it can be? It sure as Hell can't be a baby that's for one thing! The latest situation has put me in a funny mood but I don't know why? I'm neither here nor there. I'm just totally numbed by it all.

I finally get up, have a pee, feed Lacey and make myself a mug of tea and some toast and sit my arse down and try to chill-out. I can't though, the toast sticks in my throat like it has needles in it and when I attempt to wash it down with the tea I just choke. I hope this feeling doesn't last much longer; I don't want to be like this forever. If that's at all possible?

I decide to venture out and have a wander around my local town, maybe the fresh air will kick-start my brain into action? I hit the shower, dry myself, do my hair in my own style, add some make-up (only light) - although no perfume today for some reason? - and then get myself dressed.

I'm not out to impress today, my natural good looks and perfect figure will do that for me anyway, so I just put on a pair of black stretch-jeans from TK Max, a grey hoodie and a pair of white trainers, both from Cotton Traders, and then I'm ready to go.

The car park in town is surprisingly empty for a Saturday so I park up easily and hit the shops. I'm not actually out to buy anything; I just needed to get out of the flat for a while to clear my head. I make my way to a charity shop as you never know what you might find in these places, it's surprising what they sometimes throw up. Unfortunately there's nothing here that catches my eye so I head for the door to leave. Just as I get one foot out of the shop I come face to face with a rack of baby clothes and I'm immediately frozen in time and become routed to the spot. I can tell that there's going to be no getting away from any of this baby crap now or forever more.

I head back up the High Street window shopping as I go. I pass yet more charity shops, estate agents, past the town Post Office which has a queue that stretches out the main doors onto the pavement, the shitty Kebab shop that I've told you about before that's run by some dirty-looking greasy foreigner who eye-balls me in a disgusting way, and then into a smart trendy clothes shop called *Vision* that draws me in like a magnet.

Inside I'm scanned from head to toe by the two tarty-looking young girls behind the counter, both in their late-teens and chewing gum at breakneck speed. I don't stay long, the foul language from the horrendous black noise emitting from the shop speakers makes my blood boil so I have to make a run for the exit. It's no wonder that these sort-of places don't last long if this is the welcome customers receive.

At the Mini-Supermarket I pick up a wire basket and wander around filling it with stuff; a couple of bottles of white wine (German and sweet), cat food, tampons, a tube of strawberry-flavoured lubrication that costs me an horrendous £6.99!, a bunch of bananas and a bar of rum-flavoured chocolate which I adore.

I can't believe my eyes when I get to the tills. In every bloody checkout queue stand mothers with their kids, on all six checkouts! I take the shortest queue and wait behind a young attractive girl in her early-20's with her little girl sitting in the child seat of her shopping-trolley. I desperately try not to look at the kid but it's no good as she gurgles and holds out her miniature hand to me. Reluctantly I hold out one finger to her and she grabs it and starts shaking it vigorously. I can't help myself but smile back at her as her young mother turns and smiles at our connection.

"Looks like she's made a new friend" says the Mum.

But I don't want to be her friend. I don't want to be anyone's friend. I don't want to be anything. I just want to be left alone in peace.

I get the sudden urge to run out of the shop right now into the High Street and scream at anyone who dares to look at me but I don't of course. I carry on with the facade that is me, the complicated super-independent me that has the image of a Supermodel on the outside but inside I'm bruised and in utter turmoil.

Why do I feel this way? What is the reason for the way I am?

Eventually it's my turn at the till and I pay the guy - an acne-faced ginger kid of about 18 - in cash, bag up my stuff and leave.

Further down the road I walk past the town's small arcade where I spot a dirty-looking woman in her fifties wearing what looks like a shabby, dark, dirty curtain around her, including her head. She's sitting on a folding chair on the pavement trying to sell some crappy multi-cultural rag of a magazine to the passers-by, obviously without any luck. I desperately try to avoid her gaze but due to the level of people walking along the pavement around me I'm somehow levered straight into her line of fire.

"Magazine pretty lady, magazine pretty lady" she calls to me in her horrible pushy Slavic tone as she waves one of her shitty magazines in my face. How fucking dare she? How dare she even look at me, talk to me or even breathe the very same fucking air as me? Fucking bitch.

Moving my elbow hard-left I knock her poisonous arm out of my way thereby sending her stupid fucking magazine flying up in the air. She glares at me with her evil Slavic stare but says nothing, just jumping up off her fat arse to retrieve her magazine as I stride off back up the road to the car park.

Once in the car park itself I head in the direction of my car over by the back wall where unbelievably I'm accosted yet again by a foreign voice calling out to me:

"Car washer, car washer Miss."

I look around to see yet another dirty piece of scum eyeing me up and down, standing there with a bucket of water in one hand and a dirty wet rag in the other. I ignore this "thing" and walk on without replying.

I get in my car with my shopping bag and place it in the foot-well of the passenger seat. I drive away in disbelief of the crap that I have to endure in my life. What is going on? This scum is omnipresent wherever I go. There is no fucking escape for any of us now.

***

The remainder of the weekend is ruined but I have no reason as to why? I should be really happy for my sister Kate but I'm not, instead I'm terrified for her and her unborn child. If the all things I've seen today; the scum and the detritus, is magnified one-hundred times by the time the kid has grown into adulthood, then what sort of horrific World will that young person be living in? I genuinely feel sorry for the poor kid.

I wander around my flat like a bloody zombie, I haven't even opened either of the two bottles of wine I bought earlier such is my weird mood. I try to play with Lacey but all she wants to do is eat and sleep - typical cat. The TV is no good either with channel after channel of endless bloody repeats. I'm so pissed-off that I can't even be bothered to turn my computer on and enjoy myself with some porn. I just can't be happy today.

I'd given up listening to the radio years ago when the music went all shitty and manufactured so that's another non-starter as well. In the end I crack open one of the bottles of wine and go and stand on my balcony and watch the people of the World go about their business. As I stand there people-watching, a heady question suddenly enters my head as I wonder how much longer my Planet can survive carrying on the way it does? Surely it can't go on like this forever?

Tears well up in my eyes as the wine grabs hold of me and a icy chill spears its way down my body - my lovely body. I wonder why I'm blessed with a body and looks like mine? Why are some women pig-ugly and fat whereas I am truly beautiful? It's true; there is not one single fault in my entire form, I am perfect in every way. There is not one aspect of my body that can be improved upon. I am truly blessed. I am perfection itself.

My mind though is a different matter. I could quite easily jump off this balcony right here and now and it wouldn't make the slightest difference to the World. I won't do it of course; it would be a shame to waste such perfection. Looks like mine don't come along that often.

I give in to boredom and so decide to go and watch the crap on the TV after all as the wine seems to have mellowed my brain somewhat. I flick through a hundred channels of nothing until I come across one of the numerous jewellery channels selling one of the most gorgeous silver rings that I've ever seen in all my days. The female presenter - a very attractive brunette with a big gob and a nice tight body - wails on and on about the origins of every aspect of the ring including where the bloody silver was mined and by whom and all that meaningless shit. But still she doesn't actually tell me, the viewer, the bloody price. Finally, after what feels like an hour but is actually only 2-minutes, up pops the figure: £351.99! Bloody Hell!

I grab my mobile and dial the number on the screen as quickly as I can as Miss Gobby says she only has five left in stock so I had better get in fast. I make it just in time as all five rings sell-out in a matter of seconds but I don't care, I've claimed one for myself and its mine forever. It's funny how a bit of retail therapy can make me feel just that tad better.

I soon come back down to Earth with a thump when reality sets back in again. To compensate for my mood I start on the second bottle of wine as well as the chocolate. Today - Sunday - is actually even more boring than yesterday. I can't even be bothered to get up, except for a pee and to feed Lacey, so I stay in bed until 2pm drinking wine and eating the choc.

I do nothing for the rest of the day, not even having a shower or getting dressed. The day is a total write-off, as is the whole weekend.

***

It's Monday morning and I'm at work - the freak-show that is work. I sit here wondering where my bloody weekend has disappeared to yet again? I'm still in the same weird mood as I have been the last few days and will be for the next couple of weeks to come, I know it in advance. I need to use my superior willpower to overcome this mental down that I'm experiencing. I know that I'll pull through and come out stronger in the end. I just need to get a grip of myself and move on.

I really don't have anything else to say.

I am out of words.

8

Alan & Charlie

I guess we all have moments in our lives when we go a bit crazy and this is one of them. I am so bloody bored it's not true; I literally have nothing to occupy my mind and certainly not my body.

I've really had enough with that stupid dating agency and all those retards that occupy it as well so I've decided to abandon the site and move on, although I'm still in two-minds if I'm doing the right thing? There was some fit guys on there but I don't think that my heart was really in it. Anyway, I've still got Steve's number to fall back on, not that I've heard anything from him - typical guy!

I've also got that guy Alan's details from Richard's leaving party in the White Horse a few weeks ago. What a strange night that was! I really don't think I'll be going down that road again anytime soon. I still can't get it out of my head what I did although at the same time I don't regret it at all. It's taken me some while to get those thoughts and images out of my mind, especially as Jennifer and I see each other in the office every bloody day.

I don't give a shit what anyone thinks of me, whether they think I'm some sort-of crazy cat-girl, a lush or even a whore - I really don't fucking care.

Shall I give that guy Alan a call? I guess meeting him for a drink won't do any harm even though I honestly know where it will probably end up. I don't know what it is but the older I get the less and less I seem to care about my fate. Although you never know, he might actually turn out to be a nice guy?

I'm sitting on my bed naked with a bottle of vodka in one hand and my mobile and Alan's number in the other. After taking another large swig I dial him up. It rings twice and then he answers.

"Hello, Alan speaking."

"Hi Alan, it's Sarah. We met in the White Horse a while ago. I was with my friend Rachael."

"Oh yeah, I remember you, you're the blonde with the fit body."

"Yes, that's me." I say back cheekily.

"Listen, do you fancy meeting up for a drink sometime?"

"Yeah sure, when do you have in mind?"

"It's up to you really, I'm free anytime."

"Okay then, well how about right now?" he says sharply, taking me a little by surprise, although I agree anyway.

"Okay then, where and when do you want to meet?"

"Do you know Midhurst at all? I'll meet you in the Saint George's pub at about eightish if you're up for it?"

"I know Midhurst a little bit. It's not that far from me so I guess I'll see you there then?"

"Alright then girl, I'll see you later. Are you bringing you're friend with you, the big girl, or are you coming on your own?"

"No, it'll just be me. I'll see you later then okay?"

"Okay then Sarah, I'll see you later."

Oh crap! I sit there in total and complete bewilderment. What have I done now? Why the bloody Hell do I put myself in these situations? There's no telling what I've let myself in for this time? He could be some kind-of bloody rapist or axe-murderer for all I know? I do know for a fact that men don't give a shit about my intelligence or my independence or anything; all they want to do is screw me.

The vodka numbs my mind and any rational thinking; even though I'm already way over the drink-driving limit I still intend to drive to the pub. I just don't care. I'm fucked before I'm fucked.

I shower and clean myself up and then get dressed. I put on a sexy matching white lace bra and knickers from Van De Velde, a very short white skirt from ASOS, an all-white cotton waistcoat from Dapper with no blouse underneath and on my feet, my number-one blue suede platform Lola court-shoes. My hair and make-up I do in my own unique style featuring plenty of blusher to accentuate my cheekbones, strawberry-red lipstick, coal-black eye-shadow and a few squirts of *Opium* by Yves Saint Laurent and I'm killer hot.

I fall into the driver's seat of my car as I'm a little pissed to say the very least but also as horny as Hell, and I almost cum myself as I check-out my reflection in the rear-view mirror! I set off for Midhurst heading South-West and arrive there somehow and at whatever time but I don't actually remember the journey at all as my brain has turned to mush due to the vodka.

I find the Saint George easily on the main road through the town but unfortunately it doesn't have a car park so I have to dump the car in a side street and walk back around the corner, a short trip of only a couple of minutes or so - no big deal.

As I enter the pub everyone looks and recoils in unison at the stunning image that is me. I head for the bar and order myself a large gin, neat of course, from the old guy behind the counter who gorps at my tits like he's never seen anything like them in his sad old life. Alan suddenly appears from nowhere and we exchange "Hellos" and all that usual greeting crap and offers to pay for both mine and his drink, a pint of lager. After some initial small-talk we sit ourselves down next to each other really close on one of the soft comfy seats which wind their way around the perimeter of the pub. I have absolutely no fucking idea what he's saying to me; all I can hear is blah blah bloody blah!

After some time has disappeared into nowhere - I don't know how long? - we leave and head off through town on foot to Alan's place as I seem to think he invited me back there for a drink or something although I'm not really sure? The flat itself is small, dark and shadowy and to my initial thinking needs totally gutting as its old and poorly furnished. I sit my bum down on his crappy sofa and remove my shoes as my feet are bloody killing me from the brisk walk as Alan goes and fetches us a bottle of lager each from the fridge in the adjoining kitchen.

He returns and sits down close next to me and we talk about nothing. After the fresh air from the walk, even though it's another hot evening, I seem to have sobered-up a little bit and can semi-consciously make-out what's happening around me as Alan puts his left-hand on my right –breast and squeezes me. My eyes are wide with madness and I moan with pleasure and reach out with my left-hand and squeeze the bulge between his legs as he starts to flick his tongue in and out of my mouth.

He drops his bottle of lager onto the horrible carpeted floor and rips open my waistcoat with both hands to reveal my heaving mounds. Standing up he drops his jeans and pants and I lick and suck his knob and his lovely stiff shaft and I am out of control and I don't fucking care and I............. nothing.

As I suck him he suddenly calls out the word "Charlie" and the door next to the kitchen opens to reveal the other guy from the pub at Richard's leaving do who was with Alan but I didn't get his name at the time. It's Charlie.

He's completely naked and with a rock-hard hard-on and heading straight for me. I laugh at him as he pulls my hair by my pony-tail and I let Alan go and suck Charlie's cock and then back to Alan's and then I have both of their cocks in my mouth at the same time and I suck like fuck.

This is not rape, far from it. I want this. I want them both. If there were 10-guys right here now I would want all ten cocks in my mouth and I'd suck them all and swallow their cum. I am totally wasted. I am gone. I am fucked before I'm fucked. I suck and lick at them both, both their cocks and their balls and I'm in Heaven and Hell at one and the same fucking time.

While I'm playing around with Alan's cock and bollocks with my tongue, Charlie cuts up a line of coke on the glass coffee table. I'm not really that into drugs but the occasional snort works for me - "When in Rome" and all that! Charlie sniffs a line up his nose and reels back as he inhales it in. I take hold of Alan's cock with my left-hand and wank him as I dip my tongue into the white powder. It tastes weird as I've still got all the combined flavours of both Alan and Charles's dicks still on my taste-buds as well as the gin, lager and the vodka from earlier. I use my tongue to dissolve the powder around my mouth and over my teeth. When I'm almost done I go back to Alan's cock and suck it hard, using my tongue to circulate around his shaft as I blow him.

Charlie undoes my bra from behind and plays with my tits as I continue to suck-away on Alan's cock. On his knees he pulls my skirt and knickers off and fingers my vagina and my arse-hole and I love it and suck harder as I start to pant uncontrollably.

The mixture of alcohol and cocaine - although admittedly I didn't have much coke, I only did one line - hits my brain like a crashing wave, immediately making me giggle although I don't want to but I can't stop it. My hair has gone as wild as my vagina and my eyes are as wide as saucers but they're empty with the vision of death.

I moan to Charlie, who is still finger-fucking me, to give it to me properly. He pulls his fingers out and after repositioning himself behind me and after spitting on my hole, slowly slides his lovely cock into me. I almost collapse as all the muscles in my body turn to jelly as Charlie gives me anal. I drop down again on Alan's shinny cock and lick at his knob, running my tongue over and into his Japs-eye.

I feel my bum-cheeks tighten as Charlie pushes his cock in and out of my arse with increasing ferocity and inertia. The sensation is both a mixture of pain and pleasure as my back goes into a dip as he fucks my anal passage.

Alan pulls out of my mouth, strips naked and slides under me and I go down on his tool, easing it gently into my vagina. Charlie continues fucking me in the rear - which admittedly hasn't been the same since little Jennifer had her fist up it a while ago! - and it stings and pains me and I want and need more of this ritual humiliation.

We carry on like this for forever and a day until they both plop out of me and I fall back and over onto the sofa with my beautiful long legs wide apart and I laugh in madness. I collapse inwardly in ecstasy as both guys lap their tongues at my swollen twat. I grab their hair to hang-on and I cum in their mouths and they drink me and I die and I live.

I sit back on the sofa completely exhausted and demand to them that I want more cock. They both climb onto the sofa either side of me and I swallow both their knobs as they fuck-away at my mouth.

The situation is now totally out of my control.

I start to choke as they push their cocks deeper into my mouth as one but I want more, I want to choke on their cum and I want to die. I touch my tits with my left-hand as I wank myself with my right. I am totally wasted on alcohol, cocaine, cock and sex and I'm completely powerless to resist their onslaught.

Charlie is the first to cum into my mouth and I feel his jism squirt to the back of my throat, making me cough. Alan's ejaculate follows closely behind and I gag uncontrollably on their seed. Both guys empty their muck into my mouth as I play with their junk as they then pull out and leave me sitting here choking to death, wandering off to clean up. I sit down slumped on the sofa in a heap, shaking and completely fucked with their beautiful *Bukkake* dribbling down my chin onto my tits and the odorous air of spunk wedged up my nostrils.

***

I don't really know how long I actually lay there? It could have been half-an-hour or it could have been 6-hours, but the last thing I do recall is the sight of fists coming straight for my beautiful face and then everything going black.

I wake up in my car, which amazingly is still in exactly the same place where I parked it in the side street next to the pub. How I got here and when is a total blank but I awake slumped in the driver's seat in pain - pain in my face, my chest, my vagina and in my rear-end.

I slowly come to and check my watch and I can just about make out that it's 5.15am. Moaning from the pain I check my reflection in the rear view mirror but I don't recognize the person looking back at me in the glass -it's horrible. My left-eye is black and swollen as is my mouth which has lipstick and blood from my mouth smeared across the whole right-hand side of my face. It's only now that I realize that I had walked straight into a trap. Bastards.

Why didn't I see this coming? And yet maybe I did. What the fuck is wrong with me?

A nasty vision comes into my mind. This whole situation could have been far worse; I could have woken up dead.

My trust in people, what little of it I had in the first place, has by now completely vanished.

I check myself over and find that my ribs are in deep pain. I think they may be cracked or even broken? My waistcoat is undone as the buttons were ripped off at the start of our party. I also discover that my bra is missing as are my knickers. My lovely blue shoes are also missing as my feet are bare but when I look around in the car I notice that they're laying in the passenger-side footwell so I'm guessing that I must have carried them back here along with my purse (the metallic one from ASOS) and my car keys. Or maybe someone else put them here? Who knows?

I must have been completely out of my tree as I didn't feel a bloody thing when they obviously started punching me around. But how did I get back here? They couldn't have brought me back as they don't know my car or where I parked it, so I guess I must have found my own way back somehow, by instinct I guess?

I will never touch drink or drugs ever again.

Why do I have to make life harder for myself? What a stupid fucking bitch.

As for the here and now, I can't sit here all day that's for sure. I have to try to get myself home safe and sound and that means avoiding the bloody Police or having an accident. I'm bound to be still over the limit, not to mention the cocaine still flowing around in my bloodstream, but I decide to take the risk and drive home anyway.

My body says "No" but my will overcomes it as I fire-up the car's engine and slowly head home in the early morning gloom, the Sun not yet fully risen. It being Saturday, fortunately there's not much traffic to speak of and I just about manage the 30-minute drive unscathed although I'm still in great pain and also angry with myself as I pull slowly into my allotted parking space.

Indoors I try to cuddle Lacey but my ribs won't let me so I just give her a little stroke and some food and then head for the medicine cabinet in the bathroom to get some painkillers. I stand there staring at the reflection of myself in the cabinet mirror at what was once my beautiful face. What have I done to it? Will it ever be as gorgeous as it was before? I think my black-eye now looks even blacker in the glare of the cabinet light but my mouth is actually not quite as swollen as I thought it was at first glance.

I wash the pills down with a glass of water and then lay on my bed waiting for them to take effect. As they start to bite I try to put the horror of what's happened to me out of my mind. There's no point of going to the Police either, I willingly went back to Alan's flat and I knew I was going to get fucked. The fact that the other guy Charlie was there as well is inconsequential, I didn't exactly say "No" when I had both of their cocks in my mouth did I? I wanted them to fuck me and I enjoyed every minute, it was what came afterwards that's the problem. What a stupid cow.

When I awake the Sun is beating-in through the bedroom window and Lacey is dozing down by my left-thigh. My watch says its 3pm so I must have been asleep for some time and I genuinely feel a bit better now that the painkillers have kicked in, although I still feel sorry for myself but in reality I only have one person to blame in all this.

I get up, strip naked, and go and have a nice relaxing soak in the bath. I don't actually think my ribs are broken as the pain has subsided a lot by now but I still have some heavy bruising to the left-side of my chest where I've either been punched or kicked. As I've already said, it could have been considerably worse. I'd just like to know why they beat me? Why the fuck why?

The rest of the weekend is spent doing not very much at all, just lazing around the flat trying to sort myself out and recuperate. A quick trip to the local chemist was required to get myself a morning-after pill which cost me the princely sum of £24 and left me feeling a little bit sick for a short while. And that was about it really, another 2-days of my life totally written-off.

***

It's first-thing Monday morning and I'm sitting in the crowded waiting room of my Doctor's surgery. I phoned-in sick this morning at work and told that bitch Inga that I had a "personal problem" and that I wouldn't be coming in today. I don't care if she believed me or not, she's no bloody loss to me or anyone.

I'm squashed in-between an old woman who looks about 100-years old and a young mother, another typical Council type, with a baby that won't stop crying its bloody eyes out.

I've managed to cover my black-eye with make-up although its still a bit swollen, as is my mouth, but at first glance no-one would notice unless they got really up close to me and I'm not letting that happen any time soon. I've just thrown some inconsequential clothes on today so as not to draw too much attention to myself, just jeans, t-shirt, trainers and a big dark coat to hide within.

As for the bruises to my ribs I've managed to strap them up with bandages and I'm trying my hardest to ignore the still persistent pain they're giving me. Just to make my life doubly-worse, I've also got a horrible sensation and a slight discharge from my vagina. I just know that I've bloody caught something horrendous from those two bastards; it would just be my bloody luck if I have. I still cannot believe what a stupid bloody bitch I've been, I really am old enough to know better. There is a hard lesson to be learned here.

The waiting room is like a sea of people with coughing, sneezing, crying, miserable-looking humans all huddled together like fish in a tin can. It's like one big germ-ridden cess-pit of sickness. The sooner I get out of here the bloody better.

Unfortunately though I'm forced to wait forever until mercifully I'm called in to see my GP - Dr. Alexander. She's the very same doctor that I've had from the very day I was born right up to the here and now, so obviously she's seen me grow up over the years from a new-born baby into the beautiful woman that sits before her today.

After some general doctor / patient chat she asks me of my problem. I don't go into too many details with her about what happened on Friday night, just simply telling her that I'd met some guy and that our brief fling was over as quickly as it started and that I needed to get myself checked-out in case I had picked-up an STI or maybe worse. For some weird reason I even tell her that I caught him cheating on me! What a bloody liar, where do I get all this shit from?

I can tell by the expression on her face that she knows that I'm spinning her a fast one, she's only got to look at my face a bit closer to see that. I know she's not stupid, she's known me all my life thus far, but she has to go along with my story as she has no other proof; unless she sees me naked of course and there's no reason for that.

I have great respect for her as she dutifully says that she will make an appointment for me to attend an STI clinic in town. She looks at me like I'm an open book and as I go to leave she wishes me well and begs me to stay safe. A lump comes to my throat and I feel tears of emotion start to form in the corner of my eyes as her soft caring voice reaches out to me and wraps its warm arms around my life like a giant comforting blanket. I desperately want to tell her everything about myself and my life but I don't want to hurt or disgust her or for her to reject me and purge me of her professional care or love. At this very moment in time she is like my second mother, a surrogate if you like. I want to cry my eyes out and let myself go but I can't, I'm just too hard.

The appointment at the STI clinic I let breeze past my life, not even letting it register in my memory. I went of course and the result was positive, I had caught an infection just as I knew I had, although thankfully it's nothing serious like Gonorrhoea, Herpes or anything nasty like that. The clinic had proscribed me two-courses of antibiotics, one to take orally and the other I have to use internally, both of which I have to take for the next 3-months. After that I have to go back for another check-up and hopefully get the all-clear. In the mean-time of course that means no sex, not that I really feel much like it at the moment anyway. I just want to put this whole sorry business behind me and move on.

Everything that happens to us happens for a reason. We all have to be philosophical about these things, whatever they may be and their outcome. This whole episode has been a tough lesson and has left a nasty stain on my life, my character, my intelligence and my natural beauty. Not to mention the nasty knock it has had on my body. It has left me feeling contaminated.

9

Art is Everything

An event that I've been looking forward to quite literally for months is now finally imminent. It's an art exposition in Chichester showcasing four of the greatest artists of the 20th Century in retrospective in one place and for one-week only. By all accounts it's not a very big feature but nevertheless, the artists themselves certainly make up for lack of quantity with the sheer magnitude if the vision and skills of their work.

The four artists in question are Francis Bacon, Pablo Picasso, Salvador Dali and my own personal favourite - Jackson Pollock. His work just blows my mind; I seem to have a real connection with his art, even with his early pieces from the 1930's and early-1940's before he really got into doing his more famous dripping phase of his work.

Anyway, I've booked the day off work today, it's Monday, as I didn't really want to go to the opening day of the exposition last Saturday at the gallery as it would have been bloody packed solid. The very thought of rubbing shoulders with a bunch of chinless art-lovers does nothing for me. The vast majority of them don't even know what art is anyway.

As for today's look, I'm going to go full-hog on my appearance by wearing the shortest dress that I possess, a skimpy little taffeta mini-dress from Kissydress in white that is so bloody short that it barely covers my bum and has a moulded-in bust-shape to it so there's no need for me to wear a bra. I definitely think knickers are in order though as I don't want anyone catching a glimpse of my undercarriage!

I'm not bothering with tights or stocking either as my legs are beautifully tanned and smooth just as they are. On my feet I'm wearing my extra-special blue suede Lola court shoes that I bought in Chichester months ago that can turn heads just by themselves. I'm also taking my small Art Deco shell clutch-bag from Vintage Styler instead of a purse to carry my keys and money and other crap.

As for my make-up I've really pushed the boat out, featuring coal-black eye-shadow that fades to grey, orange lipstick and plenty of blusher to accentuate my sharp cheekbones and facial structure. My perfume today is *Mademoiselle* by Chanel. This is the art of being me.

Chichester itself is fairly busy when I arrive in town, and for early Monday morning the car park is pretty full but I manage to park easily enough. I strut down East Street like a cat out looking for revenge with everyone's eyes upon me; all the men and all the women, everyone. I love the attention and it starts to turn me on, it feels like I'm the star of the show.

I need to pay a cheque into the bank and so I decide to do that first before my date at the gallery. Seeing as it's still relatively early the bank isn't that full with only 3-people in front of me in the queue, but typically there's only one person serving at the counter, a really nice-looking blonde girl in her mid-twenties. The small queue moves along one place as I look around the open-plan area of the bank, standing there bored. I notice a couple of guys sitting to the right of me, both obviously employees of the bank, both of them checking-out my body and whispering to each other. Boys will be boys! An image of the pair of them fucking me hard at the same time suddenly flashes across my eyes for a millisecond just before it's time for me to move up one more place again and I have to quickly snap myself out of my fantasy.

The old guy that was in front of me, somewhere around 60-ish, is now at the counter being served. He's making a bloody song and dance about taking some money from one account and putting it in another and then withdrawing money from yet another account in cash so he can put it in his Building Society account or some such crap. I begin to get steamed-up as the old tosser is now starting to waste my time and that's a no-no in my book. Why is it I always get stuck behind some old fart every bloody time I'm in a queue for something?

After what feels like several days have passed the old bugger finally pisses-off and I glide over to the blonde girl serving. I hand over my cheque and my pre-written paying-in slip from by clutch-bag and immediately notice that when she opens her gorgeous mouth and speaks that she's not English but yet again another foreigner; possibly Swedish judging by her pretty face? She smiles politely and does her job as I then notice her name on the badge fixed to the left-breast of her blouse. With all those Z's and V's in her name she has to be yet another fucking Slav? My eyes roll back in disbelief and I sigh in muted shock at this constant infiltration. Aren't there any English people left in this fucking Country anymore?

With my transaction complete I strut out of the bank back into the High Street, turn right and head down the road to the art gallery with the whole World and his wife admiring my natural beauty as I bounce along with my air of superiority. I am super-cool and I know it and I let everyone else know it to.

As I make my way down the road some sort-of Asian guy heads straight for me walking in the opposite direction and has the bloody gall to try to stop me and ask me the time! Who the fuck does he think he is just coming up to me in the street trying to start a conversation? Don't these people have any eyes? Why the fuck would I want to converse with the likes of him? I continue on my way, totally ignoring this "person", even when he calls me an "Arrogant bitch" I still don't take the bait. He does not exist in my World.

I cross over the centre of town by Market Square and trot down West Street, past the splendour of Chichester Cathedral on my left, and then further down the road to Wewlesberg Gallery on the right where the exposition is being held. Although the exterior of the building is very old, the actual front of the gallery itself is ultra-modern with nice clean-flowing white-painted lines and smoked glass. The interior is similar, open-plan, spacious and in pure white.

By now it's 11.30am and the gallery is already fairly busy inside with quite a crowd gathered. I'd already purchased a ticket in advance so I could have walked straight in but now that I'm actually here and running somewhat late due to hold-ups there's no queue to be found at the entrance door - bloody typical!

A pretty young blonde girl sidles-up to me with a silver tray full of complementary Champagne. I take one with a "Thank You" and walk off further into gallery. I am by far and away the most beautiful female here, with so many frumpy androgynous arty-type women around me there is absolutely no competition for me at all. Even if you take into account all the waitresses, all of whom are really good-looking and younger than me, I am still the most gorgeous.

The gallery seems to be divided into four main sections with each featured artist situated in their own designated area. The first one I wander into is Picasso's, with four medium-sized paintings hanging on the walls and a few ceramic pots and plates displayed in glass cabinets in the centre of the room. The paintings are all portraits of women done in Picasso's own unique style with distorted faces and bodies and I'm somewhat amazed by their brilliant vibrant colours. The ceramic pieces are also quite cool-looking and have similar abstract patterns to each other and the paintings also. I'd love to own one of those for myself but the prices must be horrendous, there's no way I could ever afford one.

The Dali paintings in the next room are just as amazing. Seeing one of Dali's works in the flesh is an experience in itself as his warped sense of humour is pure joy. The quality of his painting is out of this World and so incredibly detailed although I'm not quite sure about some of his sculptures on display as they're a bit above my head.

I grab my third glass of Champagne from another pretty waitress who looks at me as though I've got a bloody cheek taking another glass and she's right, I do have a bloody cheek so what are you going to do about it bitch?

As I enter the third gallery I catch a glimpse of one of Francis Bacon's most iconic images staring at me from across the stark white room - a screaming Pope sitting on his golden throne in all its decadent horror. I become mesmerized by the image of the Pope's haunted expression and I liken his face to the torment that I constantly feel bubbling-away inside myself. I have to break away from its gaze as I start to sweat and my heartbeat increases to overload. I try to catch my breath and I have to turn and walk away, escaping to the next room.

I pinch my fourth Champagne from yet another good-looking waitress and sink it in one gulp in a desperate attempt to try and regain some control from my trance-like state. My breathing soon returns to some sort-of normality as I now find myself standing in the middle of the fourth room and the hard-stuff - Jackson Pollack - for me the main attraction for coming here in the first place.

A couple in their mid-50's are standing next to me taking the piss out of one of the paintings hanging on the wall; a long, narrow, seminal masterpiece of black and white drips spread along its entire length. The work is beautifully done with the black lines perfectly positioned in uniformity along the centre-line of the white. It's a work of incredible skill and patience that the two Philistines are obviously unable to see. Not only are they blind but they're stupid as well.

I look at them with the very nadir of horror at their naivety but they ignore me just as they ignore the quality of the painting - myself and it both being beautiful works of art. I start to feel the sweat beginning to bubble under my make-up and my blood-pressure starting to rise once again so I pinch my fifth glass of bubbly from the same waitress as before and down it in one as she stands there gorping at my action in disgust. I get the sudden urge to stab the boring couple in their backs right here and now in front of everyone and watch them die in agony. That would be a work of art in itself.

I find myself transported to the other end of the room; I am alone even though I'm surrounded by about twenty people who have all amalgamated into one single body. I stand there perplexed and under complete control from the overpowering vision before me - a giant, dark, moody, all-enveloping power of a painting. I feel myself being sucked into the very core of the art itself, its tentacles of emotion piercing my soul, touching the realm of the dead. I am frozen in time. I am not actually inside my body but have vacated it and find myself standing by my own side in some kind-of bizarre hallucination. I feel more dead than alive and no-one and nothing is equal to me at this very moment in time and space.

I am naked and alone, just my naked body and the painting. As if by magic I am drawn closer to its surface and then we are one. There is no me. There is no painting. I'm looking down on myself and all I can see before me is this beautiful female shape of blue, red, yellow, green, white and black in total molecularization. I am the most complete being on Earth, transcended from the image of pure beauty. I am both alive and dead at the same time. The World is at peace now.

Suddenly someone grabs my arm and I hear the words "Are you alright Miss?" and I spring back to life and reality - whatever that is? I turn and see one of the pretty waitresses by my side, expressing her concern.

"Oh, yes, yes, I'm fine thank you" I politely say back to her as I take another glass of Champagne - number six - and down half the contents.

The chill of the liquid quickly disperses my overheated state and soon brings me back down to Earth. I distract myself by moving to my left and stand before one of Pollock's earlier works, an abstract piece not dissimilar to one of Picasso's. Its of a woman portrayed in a distorted image from the mind of the painters inner-self, just as I see my own self. It's just like looking in the mirror.

Fears for my own mortality well-up inside my mind as I meld with the image burning into my eyes, an image of mass murder and pure death flashing across my screen. My brain fragments into a turgid mixture of unreality and sheer terror, the cracks resealing themselves just in time before I pass out.

I can't stand this anymore. I am out of control. I finish the remains of my drink, place my empty glass on the waitresses' tray and head for the exit and fresh air. Once back outside a wave of cool air rushes down my throat as I inhale and reacts like fire, burning me from the inside out. People in the street all stop and stare at me, not because of my beauty but because of my demeanour. I begin to feel bilious and I shake with fright, fright at the vision of my own self in another dimension looking down at me.

I try to pull myself together and regain some composure as I set off walking back up the High Street. The further I get up the road the more my breathing starts to return to normal and I begin to feel a bit more like my old self once again.

I breeze along like I'm floating on a cushion of air as I enter the car park. In the escapist cocoon that is the interior of my car I sit there for an age collecting myself until I'm ready to move off. After almost 45-minutes of peace and quiet I finally get going and head back home, back to my own little World.

***

I squeal with pleasure as I insert 2-fingers into my hole and wank myself silly and I laugh. I cum and cum and lick my own juice and I am totally fucked on Champagne, vodka, wine, life, death, blood, shit, men, women, cock, cunt and me.

I reposition myself at the foot of my bed and start to rub my wet vulva on the corner of the wooden bed frame, the ridged hardness of the polished surface feeling so lovely and smooth on my twat. As I ride the bed I play with my breasts vigorously, hurting myself on purpose. I pinch my stiff erect nipples, making them sore and red as I thrust my hips back and forth over the corner of the bed as I simultaneously suck on one of my dildo's – the solid 8-inch pink one from Ann Summers - pushing its length down my throat, making myself cough and splutter but I just don't care. I am fucked and I fuck myself.

I spin my body around so my head is pointing downwards and my bum up in the air and with my vagina still in contact with the corner of the bed.

I continue rubbing myself on the bedpost as I insert the dildo into my bum, using my glutinous saliva as its lubrication. It feels tighter than usual as my spit is not as greasy as my sex-lube but I push it in as far as I dare anyway, feeling its knob hit the boundary of my rectal passage.

I soon start to feel sick in this position when suddenly some horrible green shit chokes its way out of my mouth and onto the bedroom carpet. Undeterred, I carry on fucking myself until my arms start to ache and I just have to stop and recoup. I fall off the bed onto the floor with the dildo plopping out of my bum-hole and I start to both laugh and cry at the same time. I gulp down another slug of vodka which makes me cough when it goes down the wrong hole but I still don't care even though in reality I do. I do.

I sit up and caress my tits, spitting on them an oily mixture of vodka and saliva and wanking them against each other. It hurts but I carry on through the aching pain until I soon become bored. I scrape the goo off with my left-hand and rub it gently over my vagina and arsehole on one long motion and use my thumb to flick my clit as I wank myself whilst thinking of cock and cunt.

I cum and it soaks my hand and the carpet but I can't stop it. I go beyond my orgasm as I then try to insert my whole hand into my vagina, making me scream. I poke myself harder and I start to feel faint and I cum again, but this time it's no good and I sick myself all over my legs and my right-arm and my twat. The vomit is a watery mix of Champagne, vodka and this morning's toast. I feel like shit and I start to cry.

I have now travelled beyond being wasted and beyond any rational reasoning as I rub the vomit over my nakedness with my right-hand as my left is still semi-inserted in my box. I take another mouthful of vodka and swallow it down, closely followed by another which I spit out onto the carpet. I then pour the remaining quarter-bottle over my head and it runs down my face, down my chin and my neck and then drips onto my tits and then down to my fanny.

I stop and sit there suspended in time and motion in a pool of sick, vodka, saliva and cum with my brain completely fried. I don't think about anything as there's nothing to think about. What possibly could I think about? There is no rhyme nor reason - whatever that means?

I have a raging thirst to do something but I can't think what? The image of the two guys who I fucked and who beat me up a few months ago comes into my head. I imagine myself shooting both of them between their legs and watching them scream in agony as I stand before them laughing in their twisted faces. One of them falls to the smooth white floor of the art gallery I visited this morning and I stamp on his head with my favourite blue Lola court shoes, its heal stabbing him in the eye. There's blood everywhere and it turns me on. I'm naked and horny and I make love to myself at the sight of them bleeding to death and I laugh and love myself as I cum.

I kill the two bastards with a single shot each to their heads and laugh as their skulls explode over the beautiful polished floor. The mess and the blood becomes the gallery's latest piece of art.

At this very juncture in time they are both still alive but in reality they're already dead, they just don't know it yet.

I have no idea what the time is. It could be late-afternoon or early evening, I just don't know? I try to stand up but fall head-first onto the bed. I crawl off and make my way to the bathroom where I slowly creep into the shower and turn the water on full-blast to try and get rid of all the muck over my body, the gorgeous body that I adore more than I can say. I wash away the detritus the best I can as obviously I'm not really in the right mood or frame of mind for all this crap. Thankfully the water somehow rejuvenates me and I start to feel a little better.

I clamber out and dry myself off and head to the kitchen to make myself a nice milky mug of coffee to try and kick-start my brain. I click on the kettle, spoon some coffee into my favourite mug along with a couple of spoonfuls of sugar and go to the fridge to get some milk. I open the fridge door and stand there frozen to the spot once again, not because of the chill from the fridge on my naked body but because of the item I see there before me on the shelf - a large peeled cucumber.

I suddenly snap out of my vertical coma and collapse to my knees with a thud, hitting the floor and rolling over onto my back with my legs apart as wide as they will go. Slowly I insert the phallic vegetable into myself and scream and cry at my insanity and my pain that my gorgeous body has to endure. My decayed state of mind becomes a maelstrom whirlpool of both colour and noise as I push the cucumber further into myself and I love my huge veggie-cock and it loves me and I don't know anything anymore - I am completely lost.

The kitchen ceiling lowers itself down onto me, squashing and crushing me between it and the floor.

There is no day and there is no night.

***

I awake to the sound of my phone ringing in my ears and a blazing lightshow flickering away behind my eyelids. I scrape myself off the kitchen floor to go and answer it.

"Hello" I say in a muffled half-awake voice.

"Sarah, it's Inga. Are you okay? I was just wondering why you haven't turned up for work?"

Yes, you've guessed it; it's Inga, my bitch of a supervisor.

"What do you mean? I've got the day off" I snap back at her.

"No, you had yesterday booked off, not today. It's Tuesday today" the old cow retorts.

"What are you talking about? It's Monday today, I've had the day booked up for months."

"Sarah, I'm not going to argue with you. It's Tuesday today, it's half-past ten in the morning."

"No it isn't, it's Monday afternoon. What do you want?"

"Sarah, listen to me. It's Tuesday morning, are you coming into work or not?"

"No. I've got the day off. Leave me alone."

With that final outburst I hang up and switch the phone off. Bloody cow. What is her sodding problem? Is she on drugs or something?

I wander into the living room and switch on the TV and it bursts into life with the sights and sounds of breakfast TV on the screen before me - Tuesday's breakfast TV!

Oh shit! I've really fucked myself up on this one. I seem to have lost the rest of Monday along the way somewhere? Oh bollocks! That bitch Inga is going to fucking have my guts for garters for this one that's for sure.

I contemplate ringing her back to apologize but that would go against my policy of never saying sorry to anyone. No, fuck her. I'm not going to ring her back, she can kiss my arse. I'm taking today off as well!

10

Woods

As I'm sure you're fully aware by now, my body is of the upmost importance to me. And, as such, I try to keep it running in perfect condition at all times, except of course for my occasional bouts of drinking of which I'm fully aware of and are not as frequent as you might imagine.

Fortunately I'm blessed with being naturally tall - 5ft 10" - and slim - size 8 / 10 - and with excellent bone-structure and also being of good general health. Having said that, it takes a lot of hard bloody work to look and feel as good as I do. I've never smoked in my life and that has also helped me to stay fit and has helped retain my energy, looks and keep my skin nice and tight, clear and beautiful.

I don't really do much in the way of physical exercise though to be honest as I'm naturally as fit as a fiddle, although I did join a local gym once but I found it way too expensive and all the guys there were a real pain in the arse. I never got a moments peace in all the times I attended, they just wouldn't leave me alone and refused to take "No" for an answer.

In the end I had enough and packed it all in. The bloody women were almost as bad, talk about "If looks can kill." Jealousy doesn't even come close! Stupid bitches!

These days I tend to exercise more at home (and I don't just mean having sex!) rather than go out running or whatever. When I'm in the mood I do sit-ups, press-ups and other exercises such as using my rowing and bike machines, but my real big love - more of a passion really - is my mountain bike, I just love it.

The bike itself cost me an arm and a leg several years ago but was well worth it, I'd be lost without it. Its an English-manufactured custom-hybrid mountain bike with an all-aluminium frame, 24-speed, magnesium wheels and has full suspension. It also looks absolutely gorgeous in its silver, purple and orange paintwork.

I'm not really into joining a cycling club or any of that crap; I just do my own thing as per usual. I always wear the proper affiliated cycling gear though which actually looks rather cool and hugs my perfect figure nice and tight. Today I'm wearing a white cycling jersey from Core, black shorts from Sugoi, a pair of white carbon cycling shoes from Sidi, a pair of pearl Izumi cycling gloves, all topped-off with a white Giro Aeon helmet. Underneath I'm wearing a Wiggle shock-absorber plunge sport-bra and Agent Provocateur knickers, both in black. After several squirts of *Luxe* by Avon I'm ready to go.

Anyway, today I'm off on a bit of an adventure to get some fresh-air into my lungs. I'm taking myself off to Houghton Forest, nestled at the top of Bury Hill in West Sussex. I've loaded the bike onto its special rack on the back of my car, packed myself a light lunch of chicken and pasta in my small backpack, three cycle bottles - two with just water and one with vodka and Coke - and then I'm away heading South on the A29.

The traffic is relatively light and free-flowing and I arrive at Bury Hill car park in only half-an-hour or so and start to unload. There's quite a few other people here already with the same idea as me, mostly guys but a few girls around also which is good. I get plenty of looks as I prepare myself for the off, including a few guys that cycle past me that say "Hello" but I'm not interested in them today, this day is all about me.

I put my shoes, helmet and gloves on and glide away and a great rush of freedom encases my body as I roll along on my wheels. I head off left for the track that leads into the woods, breathing-in the beautiful natural fresh air from the trees.

My freedom is short-lived however as almost immediately I hear voices and the sound of other bikes closing-in behind me. I quickly look around to see three-guys racing up onto my tail and without a thought for anyone, least of all me; they come tearing past me at a rate of knots almost making me crash.

I shout at them "Stupid pricks" as they speed off into the distance. They turn their heads and shout back me but fortunately I don't catch what they say. They were probably a bunch of bloody gays anyway as no real red-bloodied guy would treat a girl like me in that way. Bloody faggots. I carry on despite their arrogant manner and soon settle down and start enjoying myself once again.

The track is nice and dry as it hasn't rained for a few weeks so I pick up my pace and change up a gear. I speed along quickly until I come to a small clearing overlooking the South Downs so I decide to stop and take-in the view. It's both beautiful and awesome. We have such a wonderful Country so why do so many arseholes have to try and fuck it up all the time, particularly those stupid idiots in the fucking Government?

I catch my breath as I take-in the view, have a quick drink from the vodka / Coke bottle followed by a bigger intake from one of my water bottles. I admire the vista for a little while longer and then carry on down the track, catching up with a young family all out for the day on their bikes - a couple both about my age and their two kids, a boy and a girl. My mind starts clicking-away to itself as I ride past them with a little smile and they in turn smile back at me. I'm thinking to myself that I could have easily ended up just like the mother / wife in that family - trapped - and I suddenly feel so grateful of my independence that I have a little smirk to myself.

Further around the track I spot the three selfish gays who have presumably stopped for a rest and a drink and have pulled over to one side. I'm not going to waste my time with them and pretend not to notice them as I zoom past although one of them shouts at me. Once again I fail to understand what he says but I ignore them anyway, I don't want any confrontation today, least of all with three guys in the middle of a forest, you never know what might happen? I had more than enough with those other two idiots a while ago.

I could go further down or turn right and head back up the hill as I come upon a fork in the track ahead of me. I decide to take the latter as this stretch of track really pushes me physically, especially my legs as I have to power hard back up the hill. It also tests my arms and my stamina as I really have to pull quite hard on my handlebars in order to stay in control. I power and struggle on but I don't give in to it, if I were to stop right now it would be a real bastard to get going again and get my rhythm back.

After some forty-minutes of hard grinding - although it feels like hours! - I near the summit and the trees start to thin-out. As I emerge from the darkness of their canopy back into the light it feels like I've just been reborn. I feel so alive but by now I'm also totally knackered and my belly is beginning to rumble so I decide to take a break.

There's an absolutely beautiful spot on the other side of the hill overlooking the small village of Amberley so I attempt to cross the A29 and have my lunch there. After dodging the speeding traffic I'm quickly over the road and the vision before my eyes is simply stunning; surely there cannot be a better view in the whole of the South of England than this? The vista before me makes me shiver even though the temperature is over 30-degrees today - it is simply breathtaking.

I want to have my lunch on the side of the hill so I coast the bike down out of view of all the traffic on the main road and dismount. Removing my gloves and helmet I sit down next to my bike and remove my small backpack and take out my lunch, have a large swig from the vodka / Coke bottle and I am at one with myself.

Days like this simply do not come any better; it is so peaceful it feels like I'm gliding around up in the sky looking down on Planet Earth. I feel so incredibly lucky to be me at this time right here and now - nothing and no-one can hurt me. It's such a beautiful day, there's not a cloud in the sky, just a vapour-trail from a passing jet on the way to somewhere else.

I don't care where they're off to, I am more than happy with being right here right now.

I finish my lunch and also all the contents of the vodka / Coke bottle. I didn't actually put that much vodka in the Coke as I'm driving, just enough to give myself a kick - only about a quarter of the bottle or maybe a bit more. I take a quick swig from one of my water bottles to wash my mouth out and then spit it out as I always somehow seem to sense the taste of plastic from the bottle in the water and it usually upsets my stomach.

I'm feeling so incredibly hot and sweaty and by now I also need to have a pee, so I collect myself together and head-off further downhill to the line of trees that follow the edge of the River Arun. Once there it's amazing how cool it is under the shielding of all the branches, it's also considerably quieter down here away from all the noise of the traffic on top of the hill. There is not a single stir of any kind to be heard - there is total silence. It feels like I'm the only person left alive in the whole wide World and I fall in love with it.

***

The vodka has by now introduced itself to my bloodstream and along with the blinding heat, the quiet, the pure loneliness, the beautiful views, my gorgeous bike and the reflection of my lovely self in my mind, I start to feel turned-on by my very own existence.

All of that and the persistent need to urinate means that obviously I have to remove some of my clothes but the more I think about my own naked body and the more the vodka hits me the more crazy I become.

I stand with my back up against one of the surrounding trees. I am completely naked. I touch my breasts with both hands and I gasp at the sensation. I love it and it loves me. I move my right-hand down my body over my hot skin, over my smooth pubic area to my vagina and I touch it and insert my index finger into myself. I squeal in passion but no-one can hear it, only me. I masturbate and quickly cum and I scream and then urinate over my fingers and down my legs. It's warm and wet and full of joy and love and it tickles.

I continue to rub myself slowly and gently as a small breeze suddenly wraps itself around my perfect body; it feels fantastic as am I.

Totally spent I stand there naked and alone against the tree for at least another 20-minutes before I attempt to move. When I finally do my whole body seems to creek against the punishment I've put it through today. Looking down I notice both my feet are a complete mess as I'm standing in a mud pie of dirt, urine and cum. It's a good job I packed some wipes in my backpack or I'd really be in a fix!

I clean myself up the best I can with a handful of wipes and begin to pull myself back together. I put my cycling clobber back on, have a small glug of water and head off to the right where there's a little track that runs up the side of the hill and joins onto the A29. I'm so fucking tired I feel like I'm about 80-years old as I push my bike back up the hill! There's no bloody way I have the strength to ride it up that's for sure.

A couple of cars slowly make their way past me as I struggle up the single-track lane, one coming down and one coming up. The one that comes from behind me sounds its horn as it passes, probably a male driver sounding-off at the gorgeous sight of my long legs and firm bum in my skin-tight cycling shorts - cheeky bastard!

Finally at the top of the lane at the junction with the A29 I stop for another breather and watch the traffic hurtle past me at speed, each one of them going over the maximum limit. I have to take my life in my hands as I run across the road with my bike. I jump back on and scoot back to the car park slowly as I feel totally exhausted and also a little faint as the Sun reaches its full height.

As I near my car I notice the tailgate is up on the MPV that is parked next to my Fiesta. Its owners are none other than the young family who I exchanged smiles with in the woods earlier.

The parents both say "Hi" to me as I pull up behind my car and I "Hi" back to them. The mother - who I would say is about my age but nowhere nearly as good-looking, in fact she's a bit mousy and also a good 6-inches shorter than me but fairly slim - looks at me and makes a comment:

"Are you okay? You look a bit pale."

"I'm fine thanks. I think I've over-exerted myself coming up that hill" I reply. In reality I feel like crap but I'm desperately trying to put a brave face on it as only I know the real reasons for my condition.

"Here, have one of these, it'll give you an energy boost and hopefully make you feel a bit better" says the husband - who is also shorter than me and not my type at all - as he hands me a bottle of energy drink.

I take off my gloves, helmet and backpack and open the tailgate to my own car. I prop my bike up against the side of my car, being careful not to scratch the paint of either, and then plonk myself down in the back and swallow a mouthful of their drink.

The couple introduce themselves as Graham and Anita along with the swopping of handshakes all around. Anita - if that was my name I would either change it by Deed-Poll or shoot myself! - turns to her little girl, herself probably around 8-years old or so and really pretty, telling her:

"Lilly, give the young lady one of your sweets darling."

"Young Lady" she calls me! I would bet that I'm older than her even though I look 10-years younger!

The little girl edges shyly towards me and holds out a small bag of those bloody horrible rubbery chewy things that the manufacturers laughingly call "sweets" but actually taste more like a condom! I decline the kind offer with a polite "No thanks" as I don't want to puke-up over the little love!

"You've got a bit more colour back in your cheeks now" quips husband Graham before I joke back at them with a smile:

"What I really need is a big stiff one!"

But I don't think either of them understands my sense of humour as my sexual innuendo clearly flies straight over their heads. It is true though, I do feel much better after having a sit-down and a couple of mouthfuls of their drink and I am thankful. It's really nice that some people actually do seem to care. I've tried to be caring in the past time and time again but all I've ever found was that people took advantage of my good nature so now I just don't bother anymore. Maybe I'll give it another try? Then again maybe I won't?

The couple get ready to leave and strap their kids into their respective seats in the back of their MPV and we say our "Goodbyes" and "Thank yous." I watch them drive away with all four of them waving at me with yet more smiles.

I take a few moments to get myself back together properly and then reattach my bike back onto its rack, change my shoes and then make my way out of the car park and head for home.

***

Back at my flat I unclip the bike from the rack and grab my stuff from the car. I keep my bike indoors as I don't have a shed or a garage or anywhere else to put it, only my numbered resident's car park space, so I always stash the bike in my hallway where its relatively out of the way.

I leave the rest of my stuff from today in the living room, give Lacey a kiss and a cuddle for being such a good girl and head for the kitchen. From the fridge I give her some of her food and pour myself a large glass of white wine - German of course - which I down as I watch her munch away.

Now we're both somewhat contented I strip-off naked in the kitchen and make my way to the shower. I recall what a great day it has been under the cleansing flow of hot water as it crashes against my flawless skin, it feels like Heaven and takes away all my aches and pains from today's ride. Easing off with the water I start to rub myself all over with my expensive body-wash lotion, leaving no part untouched.

Turning up the heat and the pressure once again I spray off all the soap and the bubbles and watch them disappear down the hole in the shower base between my feet. I then start on my gorgeous hair - the only hair on my entire body being that on my head - firstly shampooing and then using a separate conditioner.

A sudden chill hits me as I step out of the shower even though it has been a very hot sunny day. I dry myself off slowly using one of my giant white Egyptian towels, then wrapping a similar smaller one around my head after I've given it a good vigorous rub.

It's so fucking hot in the flat that I don't bother with any clothes for the rest of the day; no-one can see me up here on the top floor, and anyway, I don't give a shit even if they can.

11

Green Bikini

The green micro-bikini that I ordered on-line from Germany only 2-days ago falls onto the front door mat as the Postman slots it through my letterbox. I can't believe that its got here so quickly.

As part of my fitness regime, along with the cycling and my other exercises, I occasionally like to go swimming, this being the reason for ordering a new bikini. I've tried using swimsuits in the past but somehow I just find them too restricting, probably due to either the fact that my body-shape being top-heavy or maybe I just like feeling more naked in the water wearing a bikini, I don't know?

Anyway, I tear open the envelope along its sealed edge and out pops a small packet and an invoice for the princely sum of £39.99. Ripping the top off the clear plastic packet I pull out the contents, revealing the smallest tiniest bikini on Planet Earth! Its basically just three small green triangles held together with thin pieces of material that are no wider than 2-millimetres! Bloody Hell, is that it?

Once again I've had to order two different sizes, a size-8 for the bikini bottoms and a size-10 for the top, although I fail to understand why really as the whole thing is tied together using the thin strands of material?

I can't wait to try it on and check myself out in my full-length mirror, just like the narcissist I am, so I strip off naked straight away and put it on. I slip on the bottoms first and they're so small they barely have enough material in them to cover my pie! It has an inverted triangle with 3-ties on each of the top corners which connect together around the back and one that goes underneath my pussy and bum-cleavage and ties onto the top two. The top is equally as skimpy and although it covers my nipples, because of the size and firm roundness of my 36D's, it almost looks like I'm still actually topless but with green nips!

I spent plenty of time admiring myself in the mirror and the gorgeous reflection that bounces back at me. The bikini is ridiculously minimal - barely legal really! - but I don't bloody care, I look and feel so incredibly sexy. The small green triangle covering my minge looks amazing and the skimpy top practically exposes all of my gorgeous breasts even with the minimum of support; it looks like my two-girls are trying to escape! I don't actually need much support anyway; my breasts are still quite tight and firm even though I am the wrong side of thirty.

I run my hands over them and down my beautiful body, squeezing my waist and caressing my hips firmly. I'm actually a little afraid to touch myself for fear of burning my fingers! I place my left-hand on my left bum-cheek and my right between my legs over the tiny fabric of the bikini bottoms and start rubbing my clit with one finger. I move my left-hand to my mouth and wet another finger, inserting in into my anus and begin to finger-fuck it gently and I cum.

***

I've been coming to this swimming pool ever since I was a little girl, in fact when I think back how long it actually is it's something over 25-years now! Back then though it was just the local indoor pool but now they laughingly call it a "Leisure Centre" even though it is still exactly the same old pool as it always was!

Unfortunately I don't come here as often as I should, maybe only twice a month now, and that's only in the Summer months. In the Winter months I don't bother at all as I'm just not in the mood, having a swim is the last bloody thing on my mind when it's freezing cold outside.

After parking the car in their crappy pot-holed car park I head to the foyer to pay for today's swim. I can't believe the sight before me when I walk through the entrance door as there are literally hundreds of bloody kids swarming around everywhere, all shouting, screaming and running riot all over the place as their chav mothers just stand around doing nothing except chin-wagging to each other about useless crap. Some peaceful afternoon swim this is going to be!

I make my way to the pay-desk where I'm confronted by some great big fat woman the size of a house sitting behind the desk. Not exactly a good advert for fitness is she?

I wonder what she must be thinking when she sees me heading straight for her? We're at the complete opposite ends of the scale in terms of looks and everything with the vision of me and my natural beauty and her with her big rolls of fat everywhere. I bet she must be seething with hate and envy inside all that blubber? If she's so hung-up about her fatness then why doesn't she stop eating all those crisps that I notice lurking on the other side of the counter? I don't say much too her, I just pay my fee and walk off, leaving her sitting there looking at my tight rear end.

In the changing cubicle I strip and put on my new green bikini, fold away my clothes neatly in the locker, then step through the disinfectant tray and out into the pool area. As soon as I emerge into the wide open space I spot most of the brats I saw earlier are now fortunately up at the shallow end to my left having their swimming lesson - result!

From the edge of the pool I dive in head-first and swim underwater straight over to the other side, surface and take in air. Today I'm wearing water-resistant make-up so I can still look amazingly gorgeous even when swimming. I crawl over to the deep end and clamber out and sit on the edge looking pretty. After a short while of collecting myself I make my way over to the diving boards, picking the middle one of the three and diving in like a real pro. When I surface I swim the whole length of the pool down to where the kids are and then back again to the deep end. The water feels fantastic against my beautiful toned body and I can feel it working my muscles within.

I take another pit-stop and sit on the side of the pool and watch all the goings-on down the other end. I'm amazed at the general poor condition of most of the mothers and even the teachers with the kids. Out of about a dozen of them only one has a half-decent figure and she must be at least 10-years younger than me! The rest of them are all carrying far too much weight and look way older than their real ages. Why don't these women try to make a bloody effort and sort themselves out instead of walking around looking like old frumps? Why have they just let themselves go?

Just as I'm about to slip back into the water again I notice some official-looking guy wearing a blue polo-shirt and shorts, a whistle around his neck and with clipboard in hand heading in my direction. As he nears he suddenly starts to holler at me:

"Excuse me Miss." Says Mr. Official, a real jobs-worth type aged about fifty-five or so.

"Are you talking to me?" I fire back at him.

"Yes, I am talking to you. I'm sorry Miss but you can't swim down near the children, it's regulations."

"Is that a fact? And what regulations are those then? I've paid to swim here so I'm going to use all the pool." I shoot back at him.

"That's not the point, we can't have strangers down near the children in case they're harmed in some way." He fires off again.

"I'm not going to harm them. What do you think I am, some sort of fucking nutter?" I shout back at him.

By now my blood is starting to boil and I stand to face him. I always try to avoid confrontation with anyone at all costs and live in a quiet pacifistic state of being as I find things like this situation right now so incredibly petty and meaningless that it's just not worth bothering about. Life is too short for all this bullshit, especially after all the crap from the idiots I've had to work with over the years, not to mention all the grief I suffered from the "Old Man". But this guy though is really starting to get on my tits; I just can't let this one go unchecked.

He looks at my face in bewilderment, obviously somewhat surprised that such foul language could come from the mouth of someone so gorgeous? I also notice him checking-out my body - my long legs, my breasts and then back to my face.

"There's no need to swear at me young lady, I'm just doing my job." He bleats.

"Well go and do it somewhere else and leave me alone." I say to him, before he then hits me with the killer line.

"And another thing, your swimwear is completely unsuitable. This is a public pool. There have been some complaints."

Well that was it wasn't it. Talk about red-rag-to-a-bull. That one really made my hackles stand to attention.

"Oh yeah? Complaints from who, that fat bitch on the front counter I bet?" I stab back at him.

"No it wasn't actually. Some of the mothers with their children have told me that you should wear something more appropriate for this centre." Comes back his feeble response.

With that answer I set off marching down to the other end of the pool to have it out with whichever one of those bitches that had been slagging me off.

"Where do you think you're going? I haven't finished with you yet." Shouts "man-with-shorts" at me from behind as I walk off.

"Piss off and leave me alone." I turn and spit back at him.

Down at the other end of the pool the World has come to a complete halt as all the women and their snotty kids have stopped in their tracks at the unfolding situation between the old wanker and myself.

"Which one of you ugly bitches has been slagging me off?" I shout at the women in the pool. One of them, a head-strong authoritative type with a face that warrants a good slap, snaps at me and virtually repeats everything that Mr. Official has word for word.

"Now you listen to me, I'm just as entitled to use this pool as much as anyone else so if you don't like it I suggest you go and fuck yourself because obviously no-one else is going to." I scream at her.

That really shut the bitch up, stupid cow. The old guy, who by now has joined me down at the shallow end and stands next to me, is on his radio talking to someone. It's only now that I notice the word "Lifeguard" embroidered on his shirt, not that it makes any fucking difference to me.

"Miss. Harmsworth, would you tell the Police that there's a disturbance in the pool area and that I need their assistance." He whines.

Wow, that's a new one; I've never been called a "disturbance" before! And as for Miss. Harmsworth, I'm guessing she must be the big fat blob on reception?

"I suggest you cool down Miss." Says the so-called big-shot Lifeguard to me.

"Don't you fucking tell me what to do you old cunt. I'm perfectly entitled to swim in this pool just the same as anyone else. I'm not the one causing trouble; it's that old bag there." I rage, pointing at the old bag.

As if by magic - and eerily quick I must say! - fatty Miss. Harmsworth suddenly appears and waddles through the double exit doors accompanied by two Police officers, one male and one female, who both must have been on the premises already as there's no-way they could have got here that bloody quickly.

The female officer - about twenty-five or so, short, overweight, and with a pretty face but ginger - confers with Mr. Lifeguard about what the so-called disturbance is all about.

By now all the women and children - some of whom are crying - are out of the pool and are drying themselves off. I just stand there like a bloody lemon listening to the old git talking crap to the copper as then the male officer - a slim guy about the same age as his counterpart and with one of those horrible tight beards - asks me for my name and address.

I then decide to have my say regardless, I'm not afraid of the bloody Police; I've had run-ins with them in the past so I know how to handle them, especially the female one. Just because they drive a car with a flashing blue light on top doesn't mean that they're right all the time. I make my point firmly and calmly, stating the fact that I just came in here for a nice peaceful swim and that I just want to be left alone to do my own thing without any hassle or confrontation from anyone.

The ginger Policewoman stands and listens to my argument, during which I notice her taking a quick look checking-out my body as I make my stand. Amazingly the WPC seems to side with me although Mr. Lifeguard doesn't, immediately chipping-in with more instructions for yours truly to obey.

"I think it's best for everyone that you leave Miss." He pipes up.

"I'm not going anywhere. I've paid for my swim and that's exactly what I'm going to do." I spit back at him.

"I don't want you in my Leisure Centre again." He then comes back at me.

"Listen, I've been coming here for over twenty-five years and you're not going to stop me."

"I've never seen you in here before and I've worked here for 3-years."

"So what? I've never seen you before either." I argue back as then the Police woman quickly interjects:

"Okay, okay, this is not getting anyone anywhere. I think it would be a good idea Miss. Knowles if you were to leave before this situation gets any more out of hand. I understand you just came here for a quiet swim and that you possibly weren't aware of the Leisure Centre's policy regarding swimming near the schoolchildren, but you have to admit that your attire may be considered somewhat offensive to some people? It doesn't exactly leave much to the imagination does it?"

I stand there dumbfounded by what "Little Miss. Gingercopper" has just said to me, although I quickly realise that any more attacking on my part could land me further in the

I WANT

crap, or even worse, arrested, and I don't want that. I decide to err on the side of caution and retreat gracefully. There's more than one way to skin a cat as I'm not finished with this issue by a long chalk.

"Okay then, I'll leave. But I'm doing so under protest. I've done nothing wrong and you all know it."

As I say my piece I point at the WPC right in her face just to make bloody sure she understands me fully. Stupid fucking pig.

I glare at Mr. Lifeguard and the fat bitch as I turn on my heals and walk off, exit stage right. I feel everyone burning their eyes out on the gorgeous sight of my virtually bare arse as I strut and bounce away back to the changing area. That's right, take a good fucking look.

I strip and dry myself off, changing back into my clothes in mere minutes although I leave my hair still virtually wringing wet as I want to get out of here as quick as I possibly can. As I pass the reception desk I notice the Lifeguard, the fat cow and the two officers standing there talking. I throw my locker key onto the counter with a clang without bothering to say a single word and leave through the revolving exit door in disgust. Fuckers.

What a bunch of fucking arseholes! What exactly have I done wrong? Nothing. Okay, so my bikini is a bit on the skimpy side like the copper said, but anyone can see more female flesh than I was showing just by opening up a daily newspaper. That's no reason to call the bloody Police is it? And as for swimming down near those kids, so what? What did they think I was going to do to them, drown them all?

When I arrive back home I find myself in a remarkably calm frame of mind. My heartbeat isn't even pounding like you would expect it to be after all that bullshit.

Lacey purrs like crazy as I kiss and cuddle her and after several glasses of chilled white wine - with a large splash of vodka added for a little extra kick! - I'm also purring crazy as I insert my vibrator gently into my vagina and wank myself naked on the kitchen floor until I orgasm and scream and cum.

***

The date is now several months later. I'm wearing a black Baseball cap that I bought in the local market in town off of some old woman on a stall for 5-quid, a black Bomber-style jacket, black jeans, black trainers and a pair of black cycling gloves that I no-longer use. Even though the evening sky is dark by at least 4.30pm, I still need the cap to cover my face as I'm going out on a special mission later tonight.

The time is now 8.30pm and I've taken the back-roads to get to my destination as most of the main roads around here are now covered by CCTV security cameras and I don't want to get caught on any of them.

I park the car in a side street, retrieve the axe from under my tailgate carpet and head off to my target. I have to walk along one small section of the main road to get there but it being a Thursday night, dark, pissing with rain and all dressed in black, I doubt if many people will actually see me. Even if they do, what are they going to do about it?

In the car park I quickly find the car I'm after - a silver-blue coloured VW Passat estate. I take out the axe from inside my jacket and embed it with full power and a dull cracking-sound into the Lifeguards windscreen. Bastard.

I leave the weapon embedded in the glass, turn and walk away with the cool grace of the recidivist I am. I am perfectly fluid and in total control at all time - except when I'm not! All good things to those who wait, like this good girl.

The swimming pool - sorry, I mean Leisure Centre! - doesn't close until 9.30pm on a Thursday night so everyone will still happily be leisuring-away, so hopefully I haven't been seen by anyone. As I'm wearing the aforementioned gloves and I pre-wiped the axe clean beforehand, there won't be any fingerprints to nail me. Hopefully the useless cops won't have a clue as to who committed this heinous crime?

Obviously if I had done this on the very night of my encounter with the old fucker, the bloody Police would have been straight around to my door and no mistake, hence the gap in time.

Once safely back at home, the adrenalin-rush hits me like crazy and I laugh out loud to myself and hit the vodka. I strip naked and touch my tits and my vagina and drink myself to sleep on the sofa with Lacey curled up next to me all nice and warm and snug.

12

Extended Weekend

For the next few days - over the coming weekend - I'm taking myself off for a little break away from work, the flat, my home town and everyone and everything to hopefully try and recharge my batteries. A relation of work colleague Rachael owns a little thatched cottage in the Lake District, Cumbria, and so I've rented it off of them for the weekend for the subsidized sum of only £175 for the duration.

It's ages since I've been up to the Lakes, it must be knocking-on for almost 10-years now as the last time I was there was when I was with the long-term ex-boyfriend - the one that I don't ever mention. I just know it's going to be lovely to be back there once again as it's my favourite part of the country, especially if the weather's good. Actually the forecast for the coming next few days says it's going to nice, sunny and hot so bring it on!

Rachael - bless her - has also come to the rescue regarding Lacey and has agreed to come over to my flat and feed her twice a day - what a star! I was really dreading the thought of having to put her in a cat-hotel while I'm away as like her, I'm also territorial and this is my territory. At least this way I'll know that she'll be okay with Rachael and be in her own surroundings, although I still don't really like leaving her behind.

The village I'm staying in is Coniston, one of the nicest and longest Lakes in the whole of Cumbria, and one of the most beautiful too. I'm also taking my bike with me as I intend to go on a day's cycling tour around the Lake. Well, that's the plan anyway!

I WANT

I'm leaving quite early this morning - it's Thursday - so hopefully I'll miss most of the heavy traffic on the M25 and also the M6 which runs right through the centre of Cumbria itself. I estimate it should take me roughly 5 ½ -hours to get there but I'm not going to push it, just having a nice steady run is what I'm aiming for.

I'm not out dressed to kill this morning but even so I still like to look stylish, so I'm wearing a white v-neck jumper from Very, blue stretch-jeans from Next, a pair of black suedette platform Chelsea boots from Boohoo and a white cashmere poncho from Peter Hahn as it's a bit on the chilly side out as it's only 5.30am. My sexy black underwear is from Victoria's Secret whilst my perfume today is *Opium* by Yves Saint Laurent.

Being a typical girl I've packed far too much stuff. I've filled a suitcase and two bags full of clothes, shoes and other things for my trip even though I know I won't even need half of it. I've left Rachael enough cat food for Lacey along with a "Thank you" note and two bottles of wine, one white (German) and one red (French).

I loaded the car up last night as I always like to be well prepared in case of any eventualities and anyway I didn't want to be fannying-around doing it this morning. The only thing I have to load now is my bike as I didn't want some arsehole trying to pinch it overnight if I'd loaded it up then.

It's funny how Lacey always knows that something's up. She's a clever cat that's for sure as I guess that she's sensed that I'm leaving her and maybe she's worried that I won't be coming back? I would never do that of course, she means more to me than anything and I love her with all my heart. With my bike loaded up I kiss and cuddle her "Goodbye" with tears in my eyes, giving her a large helping of food to distract her from seeing me go as I then make my exit - my little love.

I appear to have timed things just right as the M25 is relatively light at this time of the morning. Give it another hour though and it'll be jammed solid that's for sure. I breeze along quickly enough and reach the junction with the M40 after some

116

30-minutes or so. I always find the M40 a lonely and somehow creepy motorway for some reason, although its much better now that there's more lighting along this road unlike several years ago when there were whole sections that were totally blind. I slide a CD into the player - Dido's first and classic album - and sing along with her for the next hour or so until I hit the outskirts of Birmingham.

From the M40 I connect to the M42 for a short while, passing Solihull and then the National Exhibition Centre, and from there I join the M6 for the straight run all the way up to Cumbria. Once past Birmingham itself I decide to take a quick break at the next motorway service station as I need to have a pee. I go for a little wander around the newsagent as well whilst I'm there and buy a copy of today's paper and some mints before heading back to the car, the pit-stop only taking some 20-minutes in total. I don't bother to get any petrol as I should be able to make the entire distance - roughly 340-miles - on one tank of gas, barring any hold-ups of course as the M6 does has a bit of a reputation for occasional snarl-ups.

For the next 3-hours or so I plod-on with my journey, taking-in the glorious countryside as I motor on. The Sun is fully out now and the light shines down on my beautiful England. I love my country so much that it makes me shiver every time I think of her.

Finally I reach Cumbria and I exit the M6 and turn left onto the A590, passing Levens Hall with its topiary gardens - all beautifully cut into weird and mysterious shapes - and on to Newby Bridge as I then head towards the South-end of Windermere, the largest Lake in the District.

Taking the A592 I skirt Windermere and head further North to Ambleside, a beautiful little picture-postcard town. From there I do a left-turn onto the A593 and head toward Coniston Village and the Lake itself. The roads on this section of Cumbria are fantastically twisty and lined with heavy stoned walls that take no prisoners if you're stupid enough to hit one!

The road winds its way straight into the village and I can't believe that it all looks pretty much the same as when I last saw it all those years ago, it is so lovely and peaceful. From Rachael's hand-drawn map I find the cottage fairly easily up a short hill and its just as what I expected and also what I need, its beautiful in every way. I can already tell that I'm going to enjoy my short stay here, I only wish now that I had booked the cottage for a while longer.

I park by the side of the cottage and walk around the corner to the local pub as that's where they hold the key for security. I quickly return with key in hand and make my way inside where I'm faced with an image of just what one would expect to see in a typical 400-year old cottage - old fashioned wooden furniture, chintz everywhere, lovely blue and white china (Spode - no crap!), a real fire place, floral-patterned curtains, the lot. None of it is my style at all - I prefer the sleek modern look, just like I am myself! - but that's not the point though, it wouldn't be correct and proper without all that old stuff would it?

Checking out the rest of the cottage and the interior is all done in pretty much the same style throughout, although the kitchen and bathroom are much more modern compared to the rest of the house.

After unloading the car, unpacking and having another pee, I decide to go for a wander down to the village and get some food and things for my stay. I'm almost shocked by the politeness of the locals as I walk down the hill to the main High Street as nearly all of them smile at me and say "Hello". Around my way if I said that to everyone I saw they would think I was mental! I feel so chilled-out already at the considerably slower and friendlier pace of life up here compared with all the hustle and bustle down South.

For such a small town I count at least five pubs, although I'm pretty sure they might be even more? I make my way to the general store and that too is exactly as I remember it from years ago, simply nothing has changed. I grab a basket and load up with milk, bread, butter, three ready-meals, some apples and a few other bits and pieces. I have actually brought some stuff with me from home including several bottles of wine and vodka so I don't really need much else for the time being.

From the store I head to the Tourist Information Centre to see if I can find some interesting places to visit while I'm up here. I did make myself an itinerary from places I found on the internet, but even so I still might find something that lights my fire in here that I missed otherwise.

After a quick nose around in there I continue to walk around the town, soon spotting a shop selling some Kendal Mint Cake for sale that I simply must have, it being one of my all-time favourite treats. I just know that most, if not all of it, will soon disappear tonight that's for sure! I pass the town museum and decide to venture inside and take a look around. I feel incredibly chilled-out as I slowly wander around looking at all the artefacts and other memorabilia on display from the surrounding area and beyond. I am totally at peace with myself and this is just what I needed, to get away from my life for a couple of days.

Out of town I decide to head down to Coniston's main attraction - the Lake itself. It's a brisk walk away but in reality not that far really and the reward when you get there is so worth it. I catch a small glimpse of her through the trees at the end of the access road next to the Bluebird Cafe and she is so beautiful that it takes my breath away. I stand there for an age taking in the full vista before me as I gaze down the entire length of the water with the Sun shimmering off its smooth glass-like surface. If only I could stay rooted to this very spot forever my whole life and my World would be completely fulfilled. But time is getting on and I have to rip myself away and head back to the cottage, mellowed by the sheer size and power of the Lake.

By now it's late-afternoon and I still haven't had anything to eat since breakfast this morning. I heat one of the ready-meals in the microwave and open one of the bottles of German white wine that I brought with me. I decide to eat al-fresco out in the back garden as it's still nice and warm outside, but no sooner do I sit my bum down on one of the patio chairs

I'm suddenly joined by a large duck that has jumped over the small wall at the side of the garden, obviously attracted by the smell of my food! I throw it a small piece of chicken which it swallows down in one long gulp and then stands there looking at me wanting more. I have to shoo it away though as I want to eat the rest of my meal in peace. Cheeky bloody thing!

All finished up, I go back inside and switch the small TV in the living room on and catch the local news programme and the weather report. There's more fine weather scheduled for the next few days so-says the weather girl, at least for the following three anyway. The fact that it's also off-peak season in the Lakes means I should be able to travel around easier than during the school holiday period as the roads around here during that time get totally grid-locked throughout the day. Fine weather and less traffic - double bonus!

I go and shower quickly and change my clothes for something a bit more classy; a beautiful white cotton blouse with a stand-up collar from The White Company, a tight black Jersey mini-tube skirt from Littlewoods and a pair of white leather strap-shoes that I found on-line in America that cost me an arm and a leg. I don't bother with any underwear as that's the way it is. I sharpen-up my make-up and add a few squirts of the same perfume that I've been wearing all day.

By now my watch has gone past 7pm so I lock the cottage up and head around the corner to the pub. There's only 3-people inside and one of those is the barmaid, a big brassy woman in her mid-fifties with a massive chest.

"Hello love, what would you like?" She asks me in her lovely Cumbrian accent.

"I'll have a pint of your local ale please." I tell her - "When in Rome" and all that - again!

She plonks my drink on the counter and I pay her the £3.45 in loose change. The liquid I'm confronted with is a dark, cloudy brew which looks like a dirty pond but when I take a sip it tastes absolutely lovely, really smooth and hoppy.

I sit myself down outside with my pint on my own in peace where I'm almost immediately joined by a big lollopy old Golden Labrador dog that throws himself down at my feet, actually covering my right-foot entirely! What is it with animals around here! The barmaid calls out to him to leave me alone but I tell her that it's okay and that I don't mind at all. I actually quite like him even though I'm a true cat lover at heart and don't care for dogs that much.

I sit there in the cooling evening air for the best part of the next 2-hours accompanied by my new-found friend - Roger the dog - and several pints of the local beer. After my third drink I pat Roger "Goodbye" and then head home to bed. It's been a long but pleasant day but I'm really knackered by now and looking forward to a good night's sleep.

***

After a lay-in until 10.45am - I was so unbelievably tired last night - I'm finally up, have tea and toast for breakfast, followed by a quick shower and then dress for the day.

Today I'm wearing a pair of tight blue jeans from Topshop with a white t-shirt from Gap and grey trainers from Cotton Traders. My underwear is in sexy yellow lace from Ultimo. I do my hair and make-up (light but also full-on, if that makes sense?) featuring peach-coloured lipstick. My perfume is *Poison* by Christian Dior.

I then head out in the car for the short trip over to Bowness-in-Windermere; not that far away as I'm going to have a look around the shops there and then take a little journey out on the steamer up the Lake, so hopefully that should be fun! Windermere is the biggest of all the Lakes in Cumbria at around 10 ½ - miles long and also the most commercial, but thankfully at this time of year it should be relatively free from all the throngs of tourists and bloody kids.

It only takes me less than half an hour to get there and I park up easily in the town's car park. I go for a slow wander around the few surrounding shops looking for something interesting to buy but I soon start to get a little bored by them, in the end only purchasing a couple of fridge-magnets and a wind-up furry mouse for Lacey in a bizarre-type shop. Over the main road I buy myself an ice-cream and a Coke and head down to take a look at the Lake and also to purchase a return-ticket to Ambleside on the steam-yacht *Teal* from the small wooden ticket office.

I then head off down the road a short way to board the steamer. A couple of guys there - both in their mid-twenties I guess? - stare at me as I strut past them licking my ice-cream provocatively, looking at them straight in their eyes. As I board the boat I turn to see them looking at my bum and my figure and my gorgeous blonde hair, whispering away to each other. Men, what are they like! My air of aloofness cancels-out any notions I may have about fucking both of them and I move on, totally ignoring them and everyone else.

I sit myself down on the wooden seats facing forwards at the bow of the boat and before long we start to motor up the Lake, leaving a plume of white smoke behind us as we go. It's another wonderful day with the Sun beating down on me and everything is perfect with the World.

I'm so glad I made this trip as I needed to get away from everything, although of course I really miss my little girl Lacey so much. Rachael did send me a text message to say that she's okay and that there's no need to worry, so at least my mind is at ease somewhat on that score.

We chug along at a steady pace, passing by Belle Isle, and soon reach Ambleside in only about 20-minutes. I disembark and make my way around the small town and its funny little shops. I'm a bit restricted on time due to the return boat journey back to Bowness so I haven't really got as much time to look around the town properly as I would have liked.

I wander past the weird and stupidly-small Bridge House where I spot a gorgeous hand-made glass fruit bowl in a factory shop that I just have to make my own. Its very expensive at nearly £200 but I don't care, I want it and that's all there is to it!

I guard it with my life on the return trip back on the steamer and also in the car back to the cottage, if I were to smash it I would never forgive myself. Its so beautiful and it becomes one of my most prized possessions.

***

I didn't do much last night, just chilled-out in front of the TV with a bottle of wine and loads of crisps! I'm up a bit earlier today at 9.25am as I'm taking myself off to a beautiful stately home near Cartmel at the Southern end of the park. It's Saturday.

Today I'm wearing a black 1950's retro-style pencil-skirt from Hell Bunny along with a gorgeous black strapless Basque from Kinkyminx. It's very tight and holds me in really firmly so there's no need for me to wear a bra today, which is good. I'm not wearing any knickers either because I don't want to or have to. I've also got my full power make-up on this morning with my hair up like I usually have it so everyone can see my beautiful sharp features, tied with a black silk bow. My perfume today is *Poison* once again. On my feet I'm wearing a pair of black ankle-boots from Justfab, they're not too high as I want to be able to walk properly without falling arse over tit!

After breakfast of tea and toast I head off South on the A593 and then take the A5084 and follow the edge of Coniston Water. It's yet another sunny day with not a cloud in the sky. I wonder how much longer can I be this lucky with the weather? Once again the Lake looks absolutely stunning in the sunlight, its surface shinning a mixture of blue and silver as I wind my way along. I decide to put my foot down and have some fun with the car although unfortunately it doesn't last very long as I suddenly come upon slow traffic ahead of me - a bloody tractor with a trailer-load of hay doing all of 5-miles-an-hour - followed by four other cars and now me. Bugger!

I turn off onto the B5278 and head for my destination, the little trip taking no more than 30-minutes or so in total. As I pull up in the public car park I notice there are quite a few cars here already and also a couple of coaches, one being full of Japanese tourists and the other obviously Americans judging by the way they're dressed and their clichéd perfect teeth!

The gardens here are so lovely, with gorgeous rolling fields to one side and beautifully kept private gardens surrounding the main house on the other. I queue up behind a group of Japanese tourists, about twenty of them or so, and I can't help but laugh to myself as to how small they are, I must be at least a foot taller than any of them! They all seem to be overtly happy and they all smile at me with big beaming grins and I can't help myself but smile back at them.

I find my own way around inside the house instead of joining one of the few tour-guided groups as I like to do my own thing - as per usual. Wandering around I explore all the different rooms, the styles, all the expensive ornaments and other nick-nacks on display until before long I've pretty much seen all there is to see.

I venture back outside into one of the small private gardens under the glare of the burning Sun. I decide to have some lunch from the house's very own tea room - a Coke and a wonderfully tasty slice of home-made lemon cake - and sit my arse down at a small table on my own looking pretty. I'm surrounded by other tables full of my fellow humans, the brash Americans with their superior know-it-all attitudes and the small and quiet Japanese. There are a few English people here as well, mainly retired couples in their sixties and seventies who keep themselves to themselves.

After some 45-minutes of observing everyone's behaviour - much to my amusement - and my lunch consumed, I take myself off for a walk around the gardens. Past the house on the right I find what looks like a stairway to Heaven featuring a small fountain midway up its rise. I pause there for a moment and for some peculiar reason begin to think about my life past and present and where it's going as I sit amongst the peaceful stillness of the overhanging trees and the sound of cascading water.

My quiet is soon shattered though by the arrival of the little Japanese people with their constant natter and the incessant clicking of their cameras. About half-a-dozen of the little Japanese girls, all in their late-teens, ask me in their broken English to have their photo taken with me. I'm somewhat surprised by their request but agree anyway, what harm can it do, it's just a bit of fun? We all stand in a line with the fountain behind us as a backdrop and put our arms around each other with me being the centre of attention. What's new?

With the pictures taken they all thank me with much bowing and hands pressed together and then off they go, scurrying away like they do! I can't help myself as I smile once again at their ever constant cheerfulness.

I take a stroll along the edge of a field that has a flock of sheep grazing in the near-distance. As I study them I feel so incredibly peaceful and calm and a wave of inner-serenity overwhelms me from the inside out. I take one last look around the gardens and end my stay. It's been yet another lovely day in such an idyllic and glorious setting that I don't really want to leave.

I start to think of my future once again and that I would really love to come and live here in the Lake's when I reach a certain age but not now though, I'm a town-girl at heart and would miss that dearly so I guess I'm just going to have to wait for my future to catch up with me.

As I head to my car I notice the group of Japanese tourists standing by their coach waiting to board. As soon as they spot me striding along at my usual fast pace they all begin to wave and call out to me in a mixture of Japanese and pidgin-English. I give them a wave back and say "Goodbye" with a few of the men in their group actually bowing to me in their own unique Japanese way! I'm really quite touched by their kindness and respect. Why can't the rest of the World be like them, just think what a better place it would be?

I make my way home back along the same route I used earlier, the traffic much heavier now with at least ten cars both in front and behind me.

Once back at the cottage I find myself in probably the best mood that I've been in for ages, possibly all bloody year in fact? I pour myself a large neat vodka and sink it in one go at my good fortune of being me and alive at this time. Nothing could better the way I'm feeling right now, not even the real and true love of any man.

After several more vodka's I start to go crazy for myself and strip naked in the living room and touch myself with my fingers, feeling the wetness of my slot. I squat down by one of the old wooden chairs and wank myself with 2-fingers of my right-hand whilst still clutching the bottle of vodka with the other.

My heartbeat doubles and I begin to shake as I pleasure myself, inserting the end of the three-quarters-full bottle of vodka into my hole and I cum myself over and into it, over my fingers and my hand. I keep thrusting away at myself even though I've now peaked as I want to push my own love further and harder until I cum once more and scream like fuck.

All spent I pull the neck of the bottle out of myself with a hollow plop and lick and drink down the mixture of vodka and my own juice. I laugh and sigh at myself for being the freest person on Planet Earth. I stand and take another swig from the bottle and touch my breasts, my pert nipples and my fanny as I love myself like no-one ever has or ever will.

For this evening I've redressed casually in blue stretch-jeans from Next, a white v-neck t-shirt from River Island that exposes my beautiful cleavage, and on my feet a pair of white trainers from Cotton Traders. Once again I haven't bothered with any underwear.

I head down the hill to the pub, one of the one's that I haven't been into before, for my evening meal and a drink or two or three. I sit outside The Black Bull in the evening heat listening to the sound of Church Beck River that runs beside the pub as I tuck into my plate of chicken, pasta and mixed vegetables, all washed down with a nice cold pint of lager.

I get plenty of looks of course - as per usual - as I sit there on my tod, both from the locals and the visitors, all obviously wondering how and why such a beautiful young woman is sitting here on her own?

After finishing my third lager I head back up the hill to the cottage and take off all my clothes and masturbate myself again whilst on my back. I use the cucumber that I bought on Thursday at the little store in the village and push it in and out of my vagina until I cum and piss myself laughing.

***

Yesterday was such a good day that I cannot remember better. I lay in bed this morning until 11am as I am so tranquil and at peace with myself that I don't feel like getting up at all. The Sun is shining at full-blast through the flimsy old curtains as I'm blessed yet again with another perfect day.

I stretch my body out as I do every morning to wake up my bones and click my toes when all of a sudden I let out an unexpected fart, making myself laugh!

I then open my legs as wide as they will go under the duvet, inserting the index finger of my right-hand into my vagina and start to wank myself slowly. It feels so good to be alive and it isn't long before my body shudders and I scream as I cum over myself. Now of course I really have to get up and clean up the mess and then go for a shower.

Downstairs I make myself some breakfast, a full-on English that will hopefully sustain me until at least this evening as it's now already gone past mid-day as I've decided to cut-out lunch altogether. As I eat I'm studying a flyer that I picked up

127

at the Information Centre in town the other day that features the remains of an ancient abbey down near Furness, so that's where I plan on going today. A day of spiritual enlightenment can't be bad, that's when I finally get my arse into gear that is!

As far as today's dress-code in concerned, I'm really going to push the boat out as I intend to wear the absolute minimum I can, and that means no underwear once again - no bra, no knickers - nothing! I've brought with me my little green Flor De Maria dress, and when I say little I'm talking about as short as is legally possible! Its actually quite stretchy and so hugs my tight body perfectly and really shows off my figure, although with no underwear I'll have to be extra careful! Shoe-wise I'm wearing my pair of tan-suede wedge button shoe-boots from AXParis which are both stylish and comfortable. After applying my full-on power-face and plenty of perfume - *Mademoiselle* by Chanel - and put my hair up as I usually have it, it's time to hit the road at long last.

Down in the town I stop off for a newspaper at the local petrol station. I slowly slide out of the car without flashing myself and go and grab a copy from the rack located in front of the shop. I venture inside to pay, there being just 2-people in the shop - one customer, a big guy of about fifty-five with a bald head and no neck - and a young girl serving who looks about twelve-years old!

The old guy burns his eyes into me. I don't think he can quite believe what he's seeing as he's obviously never clapped eyes on anyone as gorgeous or glamorous as me before! He literally just stands there scanning my body and cannot take his eyes off of me for one second! The girl behind the counter also stares at me in amazement as I make a bee-line straight for her.

"Just the paper thanks." I say to her politely as she then scans my paper on her machine and asks me for the 50p. I hand her two 20p pieces and a 10 and then turn on my heals, exiting the shop with two-pairs of eyes burning into my bum and my perfect long legs.

I speed my way down past the Lake once again along partially the same route as yesterday before heading off in the direction of Barrow-in-Furness. Joining the A590 to Ulverston I am constantly awestruck by what a beautiful country England is as I cruise along doing 65 in a 50-zone.

I soon pass the Barrow Monument on my right up on top of the hill with the wide expanse of Morecombe Bay over to my left. I then head for the Valley of Nightshade where eventually I find Furness Abbey after making a wrong turn somewhere or other. Oh well, no harm done!

I park easily in the car park before heading into the reception centre, there being quite a few people here already; one coachload full of pensioners, a few families with small children and also several couples, they being mostly of pensionable age as well.

Everyone stops and stares at me as I stand at the reception desk waiting to pay the entrance fee, including the two women manning the station, both of whom are the wrong side of sixty and both also the wrong side of size-20!

"Just one adult please." I say to the woman closest to the till as I hand her a £5-note from my purse - a Glomesh Vintage one in white metal mesh - as the other woman suddenly then pipes-up:

"That's a nice dress you're wearing. You've got a lovely figure."

"Yes, I know I have." I say back to her sarcastically as I then turn and walk off clutching my change and a free guide leaflet.

What is wrong with these women? If they had looked after themselves a bit better when they were younger then they too could have had bodies similar to mine instead of morphing into the two big fat blobs they are now.

I exit the building out the other side into the stifling mid-day sunshine to be confronted by the truly magnificent splendour of the Abbey. It really is a massive building and very impressive even though it is a 700-year old ruin. I wander slowly around in total amazement at the awesome power the ruin exudes, taking photos as I go on my Nikon DSLR. I capture some great images of the architecture with shots of the Abbey's arches, its former halls and even of some of the weird-shaped burial stones as I circle the remains of the building.

An obviously retired couple in their late-sixties walk past me as I'm taking another shot, the woman - short and plump with strange feet! - looks at me and gives me a fake smile as I sense the feeling of her extreme jealousy towards me. Her husband - tall and slim with an air of former management about him - just gorps at me expressionless as if he doesn't have any concept or understanding of either my image or my power over all men and women.

I sit myself down on the remains of a wall and take a swig from my water bottle, one of the bottles off of my bike, and watch all the people and the World as they go by. A gaggle of oldies from the coach out on a day-trip wander past me full of smiles, misery and death; and I catch their whispers about the shortness of my dress, my bust hanging out, the length of my legs and other such bitterness but the only effect it has on me is to make me laugh inwardly.

I go for another slow stroll around the site, this time in the opposite direction, before I wind my way back home. Eventually I find myself back at the beginning and the reception area so I decide to have a quick look around inside the small museum there. As I nose around looking at all the bits and pieces on display I try to avoid the eyeballs of the two big birds on the counter who are obviously talking about me judging by their manner. Haven't they got anything else to bloody do or gossip about?

After some 20-minutes of wandering around I head out and back to the car and climb in. The compressed heat inside the cockpit hits me like a slap in the face, it's so sodding hot in here that I have to sit there for a while with all the windows open to let the heat dissipate. It's like a fucking oven in here!

Just as I'm about to depart yet another coach pulls into the car park and I stop in my tracks and stare at its contents, realizing that I've just had a lucky escape - the coach is packed full of window-licking retards on a day out from the "Funny Farm". I have to try and avoid looking at them; I can't, as I don't want my vision to be contaminated by their horror. Firing the car up I speed out of the car park and head back to Coniston with the air-con set to chill.

Back at the cottage I strip, shower and re-figure my make-up - less dramatic - and then redress in the same clothes as earlier and adding a few squirts of the same perfume as before also.

I then head off down to the village for dinner to another pub - The Crown Inn - another that I haven't ventured into before. It's quite busy in here but I still manage to secure a table to myself okay and then order my food - Cumberland sausage with mash, peas and onion gravy, all washed down with a nice cold pint of lager. Lovely!

As I've already said, I decided to wear my green dress again as even though I've been wearing it most of the day it's only been a short day and anyway, if you look as fantastic as I do then you then you can do whatever the Hell you want, right?

Suddenly I spot some guy in his mid-twenties eyeballing me from another table, also sitting there on his own. I ignore him but he doesn't take the hint and struts over to me acting like Jack-the-Lad.

"Hi, would you like a drink?" He beams.

"No thanks, I've already got one." I reply, sarcastically pointing at my half-full glass in front of me as I speak.

"Do you mind if I join you? You look like you need some company." He comes back, obviously not taking "No" for an answer.

"Yes I do bloody mind actually so piss off." I hiss back at him, staring him out like a bitch.

His expression cracks from being Mr. Smooth to a look more akin to someone having just been spat in the face. Finally the bloody penny drops and off he trots with his tail between his legs and probably not much else. What is it with these guys? Just because they see an attractive girl sitting on her own they automatically seem to think that she's fair game? Well not this one. Not today. I'm on holiday and I'm the one calling the shots.

I finish up and decide to take a short walk around the village where I find myself heading for St. Andrews Church in the centre on town. It's so lovely and peaceful in the churchyard - just as you would expect really! – and also considerably cooler under the shielding canopy of the trees. I get a strange feeling of my own mortality sweep over me as I wander around looking at all the headstones, knowing that under that piece of earth there is the decaying remains of someone who was once alive and free and healthy and now they are nothing but a mixture of bones and dust. I guess that most of them are just a distant memory to some, with a number of them probably long forgotten by their families.

I wonder to myself if I'll ever end up like them? Lost and forgotten in time and buried in a hole in the ground with no-one to remember me?

***

I catch the Monday morning weather forecast and it's going to be another good day, fine and clear although not as warm as yesterday. I'm taking the bike out today for a round-trip tour of Coniston Water so I've prepared my water bottles, a back-pack with light lunch and also the bike itself for the run. I estimate the whole distance should be approximately 15-miles or so.

I'm wearing my full cycling gear today - obviously! - featuring a blue and black zip-jersey, black Lycra shorts, cycling shoes, road-gloves and aero-helmet all from Specialized - and I still look absolutely gorgeous, naturally! My underwear is a Hulala Bamboo push-up sport-bra in grey with white edging and white knickers from Ultimo. Today's perfume is *Luxe* by Avon.

All set and mounted up I free-wheel down the hill, turn right, and head to the local petrol station once again with the "12-year old" girl on the till. I just grab myself a copy of today's paper; I don't need anything else, and quickly scan the headlines.

Unsurprisingly there's more trouble in the Middle-East whilst yet another Government minister has been caught with his hand in the till - typical.

I make my way out of town along the now familiar route of the A593 heading South and then on to the A5084. I pull in at a lay-by to take in the view of the Lake and as ever she looks so beautiful. There's actually a bit more wind around today so the surface of the water is broken into ripples that shimmer in the late-morning Sun. I stand on the other side of one of those thick stone walls that feature up here and the mesmerizing movement of the water draws me into it and holds me in its vice-like grip, overpowering my emotions and bringing a small tear to my eye.

Suddenly a tractor and trailer full of bleating sheep rumbles past me and snaps me out of my dream. I take a moment to have a quick sip of water from one of my bottles before I set off once again, heading to the far South end of the water. Once there I take another rest for several minutes to view the full-length of the Lake and the vista of the 5 ½-mile stretch of water before me and then move on.

I turn left off of the B-road and make my way along the narrow water-yeat and then over Bouthrey Bridge, then turning left once again and head North. The road up this side of the Lake is way-smaller compared to the other side and usually has very little in the way of traffic but typically having said that, no sooner do I turn onto it I get plenty of noise behind me from the horn of some delivery van wanting to get past! I don't have much choice but to pull over to one side and let the idiot go.

This road up here roughly follows the edge of the Lake and there's actually not really that much to see on this side of Coniston, just a few private houses dotted along its length and that's about it. I decide to stop and go down to the water's edge and have some lunch, just at the point where Peel Island sits. I've made myself a roast chicken and pickle sandwich which tastes lovely, washed down with some Coke from my other drinks bottle that almost instantly gives me wind and makes me burp!

As I sit there contemplating life and all that crap, a small motor-boat with about half-a-dozen tourists on board passes before me going up the Lake. A few of them start waving at me so I give them a little wave back, it's a simple thing but it makes me feel so happy to be alive.

I have a quick flick though my newspaper and it's the same old shit as per usual - some Z-list so-called celebrity has been caught banging someone else's husband, a black kid has been stabbed to death in the City (again!), a child-murderer gets only 10-years in jail for killing a 3-year old girl instead of the bullet that I would gladly give him, another retail chain has gone to the wall, an overpaid black footballer has run over a child outside her school in his blinged-up 4x4 and then drives off without stopping, and a load of illegal immigrants are caught red-handed in the back of a lorry on the coast and then are allowed to escape by the Police - on purpose! The list of doom and gloom is endless and that was only the first couple of pages or so!

Sustained for now, I pack away my things and head off North once again. It really is such a lovely trip and I'm so glad I decided to bring my bike up here with me; the feeling of freedom is actually difficult to put into words but it makes me feel so liberated.

I pass by Brantwood House on my right and stop to take some pics, including a couple of the Lake and a selfie, and then carry on with my journey for another few miles or so. Before long I reach the North end of the Lake at Hawkshead Hill, turn left, and then head back South once again to Coniston village itself. Almost immediately the traffic becomes busier on the B5285 as I glide over Yewdale Bridge and then past Pier Cottage and the boat yard.

I take a quick breather by the Bluebird Cafe down by the edge of the Lake where I lock my bike up to a post and have a short stroll along the small narrow pier to its very end, taking a couple more shots of the Lake with my camera, the water still looking beautiful in the light of the afternoon Sun.

As I head back up the small road that joins the Lake with the village, a couple of retirees stroll past me hand-in-hand. They both smile and say "Hello" and I return the same. I wonder to myself if that could ever be me and my man when we're both their age? The trick of course is to find Mr. Right in the first place though, a task easier said than done.

Back in the village itself I decide to walk the rest of the way and so dismount and push the bike up the hill back to the cottage and sanctuary. Tomorrow is my last day in the Lakes already and I cannot believe that it's all over so bloody quickly. Wednesday will mean going back to work and having to face my co-workers and all their bullshit again but I don't really want to think about that right now.

I spend the evening out in the back garden having dinner, a bottle of white wine, reading the rest of the crap in today's paper and then a book that I bought along with me. I send Rachael a text to let her know that I'm okay and that I'll see her on Wednesday or Thursday all being well.

I lock up the cottage and go and have a nice long soak in the bath, taking my wine and book with me and then off to bed early at 9.35pm.

***

Tuesday, my last full day here in the Lakes, comes around far too quickly. I'm heading West today to Muncaster Castle, situated right on the coast of the North Channel. The next stretches of land further out from there being the Isle of Man, Northern Ireland and then on the other side of the pond - America.

After a quick shower and a light breakfast of tea and toast, I ready myself for the day. Although it's bright and sunny the temperature is a lot cooler than it has been these last few days with rain forecast for tomorrow and my journey back home down South - typical! I mustn't grumble though, I've been really lucky with the weather so far up here, especially for this time of the year.

Today I'm wearing a pair of blue skinny stone-wash jeans from New Look along with a low-cut cream jumper from Heidi that both show off my perfect figure to the max. On my feet I'm wearing a pair of tan suede ankle-boots, also from New Look. My underwear is a matching set of red bra and knickers from Agent Provocateur, my make-up and hair are both done in my usual style with my perfume being *Opium* by Yves Saint Laurent.

I set off heading South along my usual route past the Lake, then taking a right-turn onto the A595 which roughly follows the coast-line leading past the castle and beyond. The car sticks to the road like glue and is great fun as I blast along, another reason I will miss my time up here, as the roads twist and turn with their ever-present nasty stone walls.

I arrive at the castle in good time and park up, the place seemingly busy as there are plenty of cars and coaches here already. I head to the main entrance and pay the old woman standing in the doorway my fee and wander inside. The building itself is more like a mansion really rather than the typical image one has of a proper castle, and I make my way around the many old, dark and moody rooms. They're all just as you would expect really - a bit miserable looking.

I wander around with a group of other people, mainly Americans, being led and given a running commentary by the strange old tour guide. Every now and again he fires a question into his assembled audience and without fail the same bloody annoying American woman - in her early-fifties by the looks of her, smartly dressed and obviously well educated - is always the first to stick her scrawny arm up in the air with the answer, which, even more bloody annoyingly is always correct!

Even if I knew the answers to his stupid questions I couldn't be bloody bothered to answer them, I just don't care. And what is it with these Americans anyway? Why do they have to be so bloody smart all the time and prove that they're the best? We English are far superior than they'll ever be. At least we're not complacent like them - the tragedy that was 9 / 11 is testament to that.

I break free from the throng and go my own way, as is my want. Wandering around the many rooms I stumble across the drawing room, featuring the most fantastic ornate arched ceiling that I have ever seen. It is both elegant and beautiful and I become so transfixed by its imagery that I struggle to break myself away.

Out in the fresh air away from the castle and all the people, I take a look out over the countryside before me and the snaking water of the River Esk and the surrounding Whitefell Mountains. What a gorgeous part of the country this is, it's a view to rival anywhere in the whole of England. After a couple of clicks of my camera the image is captured forever and I move on.

I notice on the guide map that there's a winding trail to follow through and around the garden so I head off for a plod around the grounds on my own; the route being a bit tricky in places, especially with the boots I'm wearing! Once at the top I emerge at a clearing overlooking the vast stretch of water that is the North Channel and a perfectly flat beach. It takes a while for my feeble brain to register the view as it seems never-ending, either to the left or the right of me.

I make my way back down the trail through a surreal sea of bluebells, desperately trying not to fall arse-over-tit in the process!

Back in front of the house again I come across the same group of Americans from earlier. The smart-arse know-it-all woman cuts me a cold glance but I don't take the bait, she is invisible to me and I walk right by, totally ignoring her and the rest of her crowd.

There's an Owl Sanctuary around the other side of the castle so I decide to head for that and be nosey. On the way there though I'm distracted by another group of people standing around laughing at something to my left so I have to push my nose in and see what's going on. There on the grass on the other side of a low fence are half-a-dozen or so Lemurs, all lounging about in various positions with one of them laying there flat on his back with his little legs spread wide apart catching the heat from the Sun on his belly. It's such a comical sight and I can't help but laugh along with everyone else at their antics and I just have to capture the scene with a couple of shots on my camera.

Just as cute, even in their own kind-of sinister-looking way, are the birds over in the Owl Sanctuary. Some of them, especially the large Barn Owl, are absolutely beautiful and sit there frozen looking serine, strong and yet powerful at the same time. I stand there admiring them for an age, riveted as I stare into their gorgeous, big round eyes in a vain desperate attempt to make some kind-of psychic connection with them. They're way too-strong for me though and I have to walk away defeated although I find their beauty and inner strength quite humbling. I liken them to myself - they have looks that can literally kill - but with an underlining mysterious that is both intriguing and compelling.

Over on the other side of the castle there's a flying display of birds of prey taking place so I stand and watch that for a bit. Amongst the crowd are the American group once again and Mrs. Bloody Clever-Clogs. The girl doing the display - in her early-twenties and very pretty and with a nice figure, although my view of it is spoilt by her ill-fitting shitty-green coloured uniform - launches a big eagle-type bird into the sky from her arm which then proceeds to swoop around in the sky catching pieces of meat tied to the end of a long length of string that she twirls about her head. Like the owls, the bird of prey is both elegant and powerful. If I'm ever to be reincarnated, this is exactly what I want to come back as. Or maybe a cat?

After some 30-minutes the show is over and everyone disperses and wanders off in their different directions. I take one last look out across the twisting river before making my way back to the car park and the trip back to Coniston village.

I spend a quiet evening in the pub around the corner, mulling over the past few days. I've thoroughly enjoyed myself on the whole and I really don't want to face having to go home, although I know I have to and I miss Lacey so much that it hurts. What would I do without her, my love? I hate to think of such things so I order myself another pint of the local brew and try and take my mind off the subject.

With my second pint finished I say my "Goodbyes" to the barmaid, Roger the dog and the few locals in the pub and head back to the cottage. A few spots of rain start to descend from the night sky as I walk along, the forecast for tomorrow and my journey South being set for heavy rain. Despite the imminent downpour though it's still actually quite warm so I decide not to waste my final evening in the Lakes.

It's pitch-black and as quiet as a mouse out the back of the cottage although I can just about make out the silhouette of the small mountain following the edge of the neighbouring field. I climb over the low garden wall and head off into the night. The cooling air embraces and encircles my naked body, sending a shiver down my spine and I become engorged. I feel myself expand and drop and it turns me on even more and it feels so glorious that I laugh wickedly to myself.

I start to run but not for long, without a bra for support it makes my breasts hurt so I have to stop by the side of a tree. I run both my hands over its rough surface, feeling the texture of its knobby bark and the power the tree holds within. I squat down on my haunches and pee on the sacred ground, marking my territory forever in my own Neo-Paganistic ritual.

I stand and caress my tree - my lovely tree - and wince as it scratches my breasts and arms. I use my right-hand to touch my lower body and sigh deeply as I insert 2-fingers into my vagina and begin to enjoy my own love, increasing the rhythm rapidly to its final destination as I fall in love and copulate with my tree as I shudder and cum.

I try to regain control even though my taut body continues to shake as I take my radiant beauty down to the edge of the Lake itself. I slowly walk into the water, taking care not to disturb the spirits or its glass-like smoothness. The profound experience encapsulates my very soul and I feel so at one with not only myself but with Mother Earth and all its power. I reach down and scoop up a cupped-handful of water and anoint my body with it, the cool liquid clinging to my naked skin as it dribbles over my breasts and down to my belly, vagina and my beautiful long legs with all the love and blessing of its God.

Back at the cottage I shower quickly in piping-hot water, dry myself and put myself to bed with a lovely huge mug of hot milk and the biggest cheesy-grin this side of Cheshire. I snigger to myself for being me and being free to do whatever I fucking want in my own little World because this is what I am.

***

I wake the following morning to the sound of rain beating down on the small widow to my bedroom - it's absolutely pissing down! The journey home is going to be joy that's for sure.

I don't bother to shower as I'll have one when I get home, so I just have a quick wash followed by breakfast of cornflakes and a mug of tea. I'm not bothering to dress up today either, just wearing a pair of black track-suit bottoms from Simplybe, a grey biker-chick t-shirt from Cafe Press and on my feet a pair of grey walking boots, also from Simplybe. I do my hair and add light make-up along with a few squirts of *Luxe* by Avon before I start packing my holiday away, all in all which doesn't take me very long.

With my bike and bags loaded into the car I bid a sad farewell to my little cottage on the hill, to the village of Coniston and her beautiful Lake.

I gas-up with fuel at the local petrol station in town and once again it's the very same girl on duty behind the till that I've seen almost every day I've been up here. I pay my bill for the fuel, a newspaper and a Coke in cash but I don't think that she recognises me as I'm not glammed-up with my puppies out today like when we last met! Or maybe I'm wrong?

I head North back through the village and away as I head for Skelwith Bridge and then on to Ambleside as I want to go back the long way around to join the M6. I then go down past Windermere one last time before I join the motorway. In the gloom of the grey sky and the rain the scenery takes on a completely different look and it's so depressing that it makes me even sadder than having to leave.

The traffic on the M6 is a fucking nightmare even though it's only 11am, made worse by the foul weather of course. The spray coming up from the other cars and especially the lorries is horrendous so I try to keep my distance. I lose count of the number of ignorant morons driving along without any lights on in these bleak conditions - idiots.

I take it easy the rest of the way back home, the journey eventually taking me a little over 6-hours in total, although that's including a stop for a wee just South of Birmingham. Even though I've been away for less than a week, arriving back in my home town feels slightly alien too me but I'm really so glad to be back.

Finally home I park in my allotted parking space and switch off my engine with a sigh of relief that I actually made back in one piece and alive! Stepping into my flat I'm greeted by a pile of letters, a copy of the local free newspaper and then the tiny patter of feet quickly heading in my direction - it's Lacey - my love.

She meows and whoops at seeing me again and I pick her up in my arms and kiss and cuddle her like never before. She really is my whole life and my complete existence and I never want to be apart from her ever again,

I love her more than I can express. I walk around the flat with her cradled in my arms like a baby, but in reality it's way beyond that, we are both an extension of each other - physically, psychically and emotionally.

My mobile suddenly rings with a start, making both Lacey and myself jump out of our skins. It's Mum on the other end of the line.

"Sarah, have you heard the great news?" She enquires noisily.

"Heard what? I've only just got through the front door." I counter.

I didn't actually tell Mum that I was going away for an extended weekend, it's no-one's bloody business except mine.

"Kate's had the baby. She's so beautiful. Oh Sarah, you have to see her." She informs me with her typical over-excitement but I say nothing, I don't know what to say. I suppose I am happy for my sister but I have no emotion or expression. I am totally blank and devoid of any feeling.

I just chill-out for the rest of the evening; firstly having a shower to wash-away my extended weekend. I touch myself and use my fingers inside me and wank until I cum and laugh.

After a light dinner and a bottle of white wine I devour half a bar of Kendal Mint Cake that immediately transports me mentally back to the ever-beautiful Lake District, if only for a short while. The taste fills my head and heart with the wonderful memories of my trip, memories that will stay with me until my dying day.

I hit the sack early as tomorrow is another day and yes - you've guessed it - back to fucking work again.

13

Leave me Alone

I don't want to talk to or see anyone today; I just want to be left alone so I can escape from reality. I don't even know why I'm in such a foul mood in the first place? And no, before you ask, I have not been drinking!

The more that time moves on and the older I get, the more alienated I become from everyone and everything around me. No-one is fucking interested. No-one fucking cares.

I am so fucking sick and tired of being let down by people. Why can't they ever do what they say they'll do? I'm not the problem, it's other people around me that conspire to cause me trouble and grief all the bloody time.

I just wish people would stop pushing me or I'll end it all, then they'll have no-one to push. I am literally at the end of my rope. My sky is about to fall in and there's nothing I can do to stop it. What is the fucking point of being alive? I have fallen through the cracks of normal existence. I just wish it was all over.

How do I get out of this trap that I've set for myself? I know deep down that all the bad things that have happened to me are some sort-of punishment for all the fuck-ups I've committed. It's nature's retribution. It's karma.

I simply cannot carry on like this anymore and that's an absolute fact. Before long I will end up destroying myself and I really don't want to do that. I want to carry on but I don't know how? Or why? Being alive isn't singularly enough, there has to be more to life than this but what is it? Maybe the answer is on the other side of life but I'm too young for that. I want to survive but how can I under all this pressure? It's all just too much for me to take.

Something had better change and pretty soon otherwise I'm going to blow my fucking brains out, even though my instinct for self-preservation is super-strong. I know that the options on my future are limited, but does that mean I have to live like this? What are my alternatives?

I have so much life in me but also so much pain. I sometimes feel trapped in the wrong me.

There are so many things wrong with the World that I don't know where to start. Everything is falling apart. The World is disrupting into a state of chaos. It never stops with its relentless bullshit all the fucking time, it's one thing after another.

You are dead and I am alive.

***

From one bastard subject to another in my dejected state, my mind leaps onto thoughts of sex, men and relationships. I have no control at all over my sepulchral persona. I really do think I'm going insane.

Will I ever find my perfect partner? Does that person actually exist on this fucking Planet? Would I even know what to do with that person if they ever came into my life? No, I honestly don't think I would, I would probably run a mile and retreat straight back into my own private little World once again. I wonder how many more people there are in the World like me?

I'm not wearing any clothes or make-up or anything today because I don't fucking want to. I haven't even had a shower and I'm not going to either.

I think I'm going to have a heart attack but I don't. I open a bottle of chilled German white wine and drown my sorrows. I collapse onto the floor and cry. I want to die but at the same time I want to live. Lacey comes and cries along with me and I feel like shit.

I sometimes hate being me but I also love it. Why does everything always turn to crap?

Do I really exist or am I just a figment of my own imagination?

The pressure on my brain intensifies and I'm forced to lie down. With the glass in one hand and the bottle in the other they both tip and spill their contents onto the kitchen floor. I lay there in the wine for an age until my situation gets worse and I urinate myself. I don't want to and cannot move. Why the fuck should I anyway? I don't have to fucking breathe if I don't want to.

Just shut up and go away. I don't want to know anything. My mission is as unequivocal as it is necessary.

I must have order. I must have peace. I have to keep going. There is no going back now.

I am a queen and I am nothing. I am super-rich but I have no money.

I am my own God and then I'm not.

Planet Earth is benign. I live in a World controlled in conjunction with the seventh-sense, way beyond anything that you may deem to be real or even possible.

I have abandoned my Guardian Angel and will from this day onwards go my own way in life.

So sad.

My life is so sad.

And I am so fucking tired.

How can I carry on?

14

Christmas

I don't know what it is about this time of the year but I always have mixed feelings about Christmas. Being an atheist myself it doesn't really mean anything to me anyway. I enjoy the break from work of course -who doesn't? - but it always seems to bring nasty memories flooding back of when I was a child and the endless arguments between my parents when we were all living in the "Family" home - a warzone. All the turmoil with my so-called "Father" constantly reducing Mum to tears with his increasingly worsening schizoid behaviour and bullying attitude, and with me and my sister Kate caught up in the middle of it all.

Arguments and tears, that's all I remember.

They were terrible times and of course it had its effects on all of us, all to varying degrees. For me personally though, the way I am now and the attitude I have on life and those around me largely stems from that horror, transforming me into what I have become today.

Why is it that the bad days always outweigh the good? The abuse he gave me was mental, ever-lasting and far worse than the physical kind.

That cannot be the sum total of my childhood can it? Why is it that some kids have a happy family life whereas others like me get the shitty end of the stick? Life simply isn't fair.

Will I ever be free of the past? The past of one's life is intrinsically linked to the present and therefore the future and there's nothing anyone can do about it. That doesn't make it any easier of course; in fact it makes it a damn sight worse as far as I'm concerned. This isn't an excuse for my actions you understand, neither am I requesting violins; I'm just underlining my continuing living nightmare.

I remember one fateful night - I think it was about 1 or 2-o'clock in the morning if I remember correctly? - when I was about 14-years old or so, and I had sneaked out of my bedroom to go for a quick pee. I was completely naked at the time and as I was a young developer I already had a beautiful figure - I was also shaving my lady-garden by then as well - when I was suddenly confronted with the awful sight of the "Old Man" standing before me in the hallway. He was also totally naked, but to make the situation worse he also had a great big hard-on as well! We both stood there frozen in each other's shocked gaze for what seemed like ages but must in fact have only been a few seconds at the most before I hurried back to my room.

What the Hell was he doing standing there like that at that time of the bloody morning? I'd really rather not think about the answer. I still to this very day cannot get that terrible image out of my head. That one defining moment was the prequel to my future torment by him and I have suffered ever since. The way he treated me will be with me forever. I will always be tarnished. He knocked the confidence out of me and gave me this cynical outlook on life that I am forever cursed with.

Strangely he only ever laid his hands on me the one time. It was the very same night that he put a knife to my throat and told me he was going to kill me. We had had a stupid trivial argument over who was going to watch whatever program on the TV when he suddenly snapped and went crazy, and that's what led to the knife incident. Fortunately Mum was there and stepped-in between us and managed to calm him down. It didn't last of course as the very next day he threw me out of the house.

It was perfect timing on his part; I had just been made redundant for the first time so I was already at a low point. In the end though he couldn't legally get rid of me as the family home was jointly owned between both my parents so I found myself caught in the middle of a stalemate. The old bugger therefore needed Mum's permission to extricate me, something that she wasn't prepared to do.

Having said that, I will never forget her bowing-down to him at first like the dutiful subservient wife that she was back then so it was a bit touch-and-go for a short while as to whether I was actually "in" or "out" of the house. That hesitant betrayal on her part is something that I've never forgotten or forgiven her for and it still sticks in my side even to this day.

Mum told me a while ago that sometime after I'd actually left home, it late one night (it always is isn't it?) when she heard some kind-of disturbance out in the back garden. When she peered out of her bedroom window - Mum had moved into my old room when I departed as the cracks in my parents' marriage had gotten considerably worse - she caught the "Old Man" standing there wanking-off over the plants in the garden! What a weirdo! They were definitely strange times and I hated every second of it.

I had also caught him several times myself stealing things from my bedroom - books, magazines and other stuff. Not because he wanted them as usually he threw them out with the rubbish, but because he was fucking mental.

Also, if one of us girls was in the toilet and he needed to use it he would stand outside the bathroom door flicking the light-switch on and off. Then he would start playing around with the door handle by constantly trying to open it, supposedly trying to make us hurry up. When the three of us ignored him that just made him even madder, which in turn made the whole situation spiral more and more out of control.

To escape his wrath I discovered the healing powers of alcohol and music - alcohol to numb the pain and music as a method of escape. It was the words of David Bowie that gave me independence and the power of Punk and the darkness of Goth that gave me a sense of belonging and hope in this fucking shitty World.

Him punishing me just for existing made me hard - maybe too hard one might say? - but either way, it has given me the strength to combat anything that anyone dares throw at me. Because of his rejection I withdrew further into myself and closed the door behind me. I now find myself alone whilst coupled with a wanting need for love - of any kind.

That old saying "You can choose your friends but you can't choose your family" is a load of old crap. You can choose whoever you bloody-well like in life. It's your choice. Use it.

Voices and words from the past fill my head as I try so hard to remember the good times. There aren't any.

As has become the norm over the years, Kate and I usually spend Christmas Day at Mums but this year things are going to different as we're both staying at Mums house from Christmas Eve to the morning after Boxing Day, well I am anyway. I guess it will make a nice change but I do have reservations about how it's all going to turn out, especially as there will be the four of us now with baby Abigail. Gary - Kate's useless boyfriend - is fortunately not on the scene anymore so at least he won't be there to spoil everything. At least he's finally got his finger out and got himself another job at last and is providing some money for the kid. Just as he bloody-well should do.

There's also the added complication with my cat Lacey as she's coming with me to Mum's. I've absolutely no intention of putting her in a cat-home over the break, that wouldn't do either of us any good as we just couldn't bear to be apart even for a few days. Mum also has a cat of her own - Suzie - who at nearly twenty-years old is getting on a bit it must be said. It remains to be seen how the two cats will get along with each other, never mind the three of us women and a baby! I really do hope little Abigail doesn't scream her head off all the bloody time. If there's one thing in life I can't bloody stand it's the sound of a screaming baby, the noise just seems to rattle around inside my head like a pea in a tin can and it drives me completely insane.

Subconsciously I guess this is one of the reasons why I don't have any kids. Yet? Never? Ever?

I hope I've packed enough clothes and things for the Christmas break, if not then it's just too bad. I load the car up first before having to deal with trying to coax Lacey into her cat-box. I dupe her with some of her favourite cat-bites - Dreamies - and in she wanders unaware of my trick, bless!

I've dressed quite sharp today as I want to make a bit of a statement when I turn up at Mum's, they both know I'm beautiful but I just want to underline the fact. I'm wearing a blue silk blouse from French Connection that I've left the buttons open lower than anyone else would dare to go, an animal-print pencil skirt from ASOS and my blue Lola platform "Chichester" court shoes. My underwear is from Ann Summers in sexy red lace and my perfume is *Mademoiselle* by Chanel.

I lock-up the flat and with Lacey in hand we make our way downstairs, although no sooner do I step out of the main lobby door to my block I come face to face with one of the Rubbish-Bin men (sorry, I mean Refuse Operatives!) as he suddenly blurts-out to me:

"Good morning Miss, I'm collecting for our Christmas Box."

"What?" I fire back at him.

"Our Christmas Box" He replies.

"Christmas Box? What are you talking about?"

"We're collecting money for Christmas, tips for all the operatives."

"You mean you want me to give you money?" I enquire.

"Well, yes." He bleats back.

"What for, don't you get wages?" I stab.

"Yes, of course we do, but this is for Christmas."

"Are you for real?"

"What do you mean?"

"I pay your wages through my Council Tax and you expect me to give you cash on the side just because it's Christmas? Are you taking the piss?"

"Well, all the other residents have given us tips." He whines pathetically.

150

"Do I look like any of the other residents?" I quiz him back.

"Well, no." He bleats.

"No, exactly. That's because I'm not. No-one gives me tips just because it's Christmas at my workplace so why should I give anything to you?"

"Because it's Christmas." He bleats at me again.

"You've got to be fucking joking?" I say to him as I glare into his stupid eyes before walking off in disgust over to my car. Unbelievable, what a bloody cheek!

Mum's house is only some twenty to thirty-minutes' drive away and I arrive there only to find that Kate and the baby are already here as her car is parked in Mum's driveway. I really hate coming back to my home town; it always seems to look smaller and dirtier every time I come here. The houses are more akin to rabbit hutches in size than anything else! All the bloody foreigners around here don't help the situation either, they just disgust me, my town has become violated.

I have to park outside the house in the road as there's not enough room on the driveway for three cars with Mum's obviously being there as well. Just as I get out of the car a menacing figure dressed all in black that looks like a walking letterbox shuffles past me going in the opposite direction. It's another bloody foreigner. Now where did I put my gun?

I carry Lacey in her box to the front door where we're both greeted by Mum standing there waiting. She takes her in-hand as I go back and retrieve my things from the car and lock it. Inside the house it's lovely and warm with Christmas decorations dotted about the hallway, not too over the top. That is except for the Christmas tree in the living room which is completely plastered with stuff all over and below in Mum's usual extravagant way.

I say "Hi" to Kate and baby Abigail as I let Lacey out of her box, virtually having to tip it on its end in order to extract her! Mum's cat Suzie is fast asleep on the arm of the sofa completely oblivious to the intrusion and doesn't bat an eyelid although I doubt that things will stay this calm for very long?

As I make a little fuss of Abigail, taking her hand and playing with her miniature fingers, Mum suddenly launches into one of her strikes at me with another of her stupid comments:

"You could have one of those when you decide to settle down."

Oh please!

"Mum, for Christ sake! I've just walked through the bloody door; don't start on me already with the same old crap you always come out with" I spit back at her in disgust and retaliation.

"She's only saying Sarah, give it a rest" Kate then chips in.

"Look, I've only just bloody got here so don't the two of you start on me already with the usual baby / boyfriend / marriage crap or I'm off home okay?" I spit back at them.

The atmosphere has already turned sour in the space of only 5-minutes and I'm ready to walk out the door right now until Mum steps-in with an offer of a drink. Both Kate and I accept in unison and the tension is somewhat doused, for now anyway.

I make my way upstairs to one of the spare bedrooms and put my bags on the bed. I'll leave the unpacking to later as I need to get some alcohol inside me and loosen myself up, so I head straight back downstairs for a glass or two or three of wine or hopefully something stronger.

I park my sweet arse in an armchair with Lacey immediately jumping up onto my lap and sitting herself down, purring away as she does. The atmosphere seems much better now, pleasant even, as the air becomes a bit more settled. Maybe this wasn't such a bad idea after all?

A short while later I help Mum in the kitchen with preparing the dinner, we're only eating light as tomorrow we're having a full-on Christmas spread - a real blow-out. For dinner today though we're having cold chicken with chips and a mixed salad, all washed down with yet more wine. Kate tends to Abigail and also the two cats who are both a bit more lively now that it's time for food, amazingly they seem to be behaving themselves together!

Later - by now it's 8pm - we all settle ourselves down in the living room to watch TV although Mum has the bloody volume up so loud I can't hear myself think. I could shout at her at the top of my voice but she still wouldn't hear me! When she eventually twigs to the din she proceeds to turn the volume down so low that we all have to sit there struggling to hear it! You just can't win!

Incredibly the two cats have both gone to sleep together in Suzie's basket and look so peaceful that I just have to take a photo of them on my phone, a beautiful picture that I will treasure forever.

Kate goes and puts little Abigail down in her bedroom, the one right next to mine, as she's already gone off to sleep and returns to us after only a few minutes. Mum and her loose themselves in a film that's on the box but I just sit there bored and tired and in a reflecting mood, reflecting on yet another year that's about to come to an end and my involvement within it. I guess it hasn't been a bad year on the whole; I got myself into a few scrapes, particularly with those two idiots who punched me around. That episode certainly could have been a whole lot worse that's for sure.

But have I moved on in my life? Am I a better person? Am I worse? Where do I go from here? What will the New Year bring me? Will it be better or worse? Whatever is going to happen next year it has to be "My" year, it has to be, doesn't it? Although if I could predict my future I would probably have to kill myself right here and now in order to save myself any more pain. All these thoughts and images make me sick to my stomach and I pour myself another glass of wine and take a huge gulp.

For some reason I start to think about work and what the Hell am I going to do about it? Should I stay there or look for something else? I think at the present moment it's a case of "Better the Devil you know" so I think I'll stay put for the time being. I have to tell you though, in the week leading up to Christmas, some of my office co-workers - or "Lemmings" as

I call them - got together for their own little works do, not an official office party. As per bloody usual I wasn't invited, not that I would have gone anyway as it was just for all the old farts in my department, I would have been bored out of my bloody skull anyway. Even so, it would have been nice to have been asked for once. I did hear on the grape-vine though that that fucking Polish bitch Irenka had somehow muscled her way into going - typical. Bloody creepy pasty-faced dead-eyed Slav bitch.

Apparently there was no official company party due to cutbacks, so they say? I find that a bit strange seeing that the company still managed to purchase brand new BMW's for all the directors somehow? Odd that isn't it? I bet they all received nice big fat Christmas bonuses as well? Bastards.

My mind takes a further downward turn as I remember one fateful event at Christmas years ago when I was with the ex-boyfriend, the one that cannot be named. I had a pregnancy scare having missed two periods so obviously I automatically thought the worst. However, the lateness was put down to stress by my Doctor, caused by the "Old Man" and his attitude towards me coupled with the ex having asked me to marry him a couple of months previously. I couldn't go through with it of course, which once again made the whole situation far worse and escalated the problem out of control.

The film on TV is one we've all seen a million times and I've had enough of it so I decide to hit the sack, even though it hasn't finished yet and it's only 10.20pm. My reminiscing has destroyed the ending of my day and so I say "Goodnight" to Mum and Kate, take Lacey in my arms and head off upstairs to bed.

***

It's 1.20am the following morning - Christmas morning - and I'm woken by the sound of distant rumbling. I turn over onto my back to try to make out what it is that's making the noise and I don't believe it - it's Mum snoring her bloody head off!

This is no good; I can't lie here all night listening to this crap. I get up and creep along naked in the dark to Mum's bedroom where I find that she's left her door ajar. In a loud whisper I tell her to "Stop bloody snoring" and she moans and turns over - peace at last. I slowly clamber back into bed, trying not to disturb Lacey in the process, and attempt to get back to sleep, back to dream.

It's 1.35am and the whole of England is shaken out of their beds by the awakening of Abigail and her little pair of lungs crying and wailing out loud like a siren in a still city street. I hear her being attended to by both Kate and Mum and now the whole house is awake, not that I was asleep anyway, it being only fifteen-minutes since the last disruption. I just lay there stroking Lacey, desperately trying to keep her calm and from getting involved in the melee.

A good half-an-hour passes until all is quiet again but by this time I'm totally awake and the cogs in my mind are whizzing around at full speed. I eventually begin to drift away and I must have nodded off as when I'm woken up for the third time it's now 4.30am; it's Mum yet again with yet more bloody snoring.

I've completely had enough of this by now so I get up and go for a pee. Sitting there on the loo actually helps to clear my mind a little but doesn't stop the grunting noises emulating from Mum's gob. Once finished I repeat the previous performance by telling her to "Shut up" and then head back to bed and try to settle myself down.

It's 5.55am and Abigail, the brat, is off on her merry (Merry Christmas!) way once again. This time I've really had enough and thoughts of leaving the house right here and now take me over but I don't really want to spend Christmas Day on my own. Anyway, there's no food back at my place and I don't want to cook even if there was. I start to think about Steve and wonder what he's doing? I guess he's still asleep and laying there in his bed all nice and warm, lovely and cosy. I wish I was there with him, touching him, with him holding me in his arms like a man does. I think I love him, although I'm not absolutely sure what love feels like anymore?

With the latest fracas seemingly over some 20-minutes later, I doze but I don't sleep, it's too late for that now - or do I mean too early? Either way I decide to stay on and see the day through, mainly because I couldn't be bothered to do anything else.

At 9.30am I get up, have another pee, clean my teeth, put on my night robe - the black silk Julianne Coco one from Figleaves - and make my way downstairs with my brain dazed by the lack of sleep. I fucking hate having my sleep disrupted - for whatever reason. The smell of toast hits me as I near the kitchen where I find Mum munching away and Kate giving Abigail some milk from a bottle. Over in the corner the two cats are both eating their breakfasts like their lives depended on it.

"Here she is! You managed to sleep through Abi crying then?" says Mum, who I always think is being sarcastic but I know in reality that she just doesn't think like me.

"No, I heard her alright." I reply.

"Well why didn't you get up then?" she cuts back at me.

"And what exactly do you expect me to do? It doesn't take 3-people to feed one baby does it?" I snap back at her.

Over the years I've learned to always be on the defensive as I'm always being attacked in one way or another, leading me to become hard, sometimes maybe too hard. I also notice that I didn't get a "Good Morning" or even a "Merry Bloody Christmas" from either Mum or Kate so I don't bother saying it to them. It's funny how Mum has changed (it isn't really) from that mild and meek woman when we were kids into the hard-nosed cow that she is today.

There's also no point in mentioning last night's snoring episode either as A: she wouldn't believe me, and B: if by some miracle she did actually believe me all I would receive in reply is denial followed by a mouthful of abuse. I didn't expect an apology anyway and none was forthcoming, which once again is just bloody typical of Mum's latter-life attitude.

I squat down and kiss and cuddle the two cats and wish them both a "Happy Christmas" and then stick the toaster back on and make myself a cup of tea. We all have the remains of breakfast together but the mood is dark and I still really want to go home, back to my flat, back to my sanctuary.

I shower and then dress for the day, nothing to elaborate, just a nice white shirt and a pair of blue skinny-jeans, both from Next. My underwear is from Ultimo in white lace and my perfume is *Poison* by Christian Dior. There's no need to wear anything else as Mum has the heating up so high it's like the bloody Tropics in here!

With everyone all dressed for the day the three of us girls all muck-in together in preparing the Christmas dinner. We're having roast lamb as none of us particularly like turkey, not even the two cats. Along with the lamb we prepare chipolata sausages, roast potatoes, sprouts (it's actually illegal not to have them at Christmas!), carrots and parsnips, all covered in Mum's special gravy and plenty of mint sauce. As for drink, I've brought along with me 4-bottles of my favourite German white wine which is chilling-away nicely in the fridge.

For afters, Mum has homemade us one of her Christmas puds which are always lovely, especially with a large dollop of brandy butter on top and plenty of cream as well, bugger the waistline!

As the dinner cooks itself we while away the time with more TV. I can't believe how bad the TV programmes are at Christmas, even worse than last year and that's saying something! They're even worse than the rest of the bloody year, they're that bad! It's the same old crap year after year, over and over again, year in year out. There's not even a decent film on except for one late tonight at 11.30pm which is no bloody good as most people will be pissed out of their skulls by then! And if I hear that fucking Christmas song by Slade one more bloody time I'm going to go insane!

We prepare the dining table and it looks lovely, so much so it almost makes me cry for some weird reason and I have to quietly retreat to the living room to see Lacey and Suzie to calm myself down, giving them lots of kisses and attention.

Almost 2-hours later and we're ready to go with the three of us plating-up together and we all tuck in. Mum, Kate and myself, not forgetting little baby Abigail and the two cats - I must admit here and now - have a wonderful Christmas feast; lots of great food, wine, laughter, family, pets, presents, even some sadness and a few tears thrown in for good measure. All in all it turns out to be a lovely day.

I go to bed early at 10.15pm due to the lack of sleep the night before and too much wine (again!) but it's to no avail, I have another restless night full of tossing and turning and featuring more snoring and bawling and far too much thinking.

**

It's Boxing Day and I don't emerge from my bed until 11am. Mum and Kate are already up and ready for the day ahead but I'm not so I take my bloody time. I hit the shower and wank myself as the hot water splashes down on my perfect body. I lay on my back with my long legs in the air and let the water slap against my hole and I cum quickly and yelp and I love it and laugh.

Before going down to breakfast I dress for the day. I'm wearing a cream-coloured low-cut v-neck lace sleeveless top and blue Rochelle high-waisted skinny jeans, both from BooHoo, and no underwear at all as I'm clear for the next few weeks and also I like to feel the sensation of the fabric over my firm body. I've got my hair up in a pony-tail as per usual and a little more make-up on today than yesterday featuring orange lipstick as I just felt like it. My perfume is *Luxe* by Avon.

Once again the day passes relatively smoothly - mainly eating, drinking and more crap TV (featuring that bloody Slade song yet again!) - with only a few smart comments from Mum and Kate against yours truly that I counter easily, more of the same old crap about boyfriends / kids / drinking too much blah blah blah, mixed in with "Why aren't you wearing a bra?" and "Your top is too revealing" and all that shit. I really try not to take it all to heart but subconsciously I know that I do.

I'm so bloody tired at the end of the day that I head off to bed at 9.15pm. Not only tired, but I'm secretly wishing the day away as I really want to go back home to my flat as I've had enough by now. I don't think I could have gotten this far without bringing Lacey with me; she's my only real friend.

Fortunately Boxing Day night passes by quicker and less disruptive than the previous two with no snoring this time, although little Abigail had me awake a couple of times with her crying. The morning comes and I'm up and out of bed at 9.15am and I'm as happy as a pig in shit as today I'm going home! I shower and touch myself and I'm in such a good mood, I feel as great as I look. I dress in the same clothes as yesterday - I don't know why as I brought loads of clothes with me? - even using the same perfume and doing my hair and make-up all exactly as before.

We all breakfast together and there's a lovely warm feeling of being part of a real family that surrounds me, a real sense of love and connection. We finish-up and both Kate and I pack our respective things ready for our journey home, she with little Abigail and myself with Lacey, and before long it's 11.30am and time for us to depart.

The whole Christmas event has been far less painful than I expected, but in reality two full-on days and three fractured nights was more than enough for me. Kate and I say our "Goodbyes" but Mum seems a bit distant and almost tearful at our leaving, but at the end of the day we're all grown women now with our own individual lives. Time and life have both moved on and that's the way it is.

*****

It really is so good to be home once again and it feels like a great big weight has been lifted off of me. There is absolutely no pressure here and I'm totally at peace with myself and everything.

I feed Lacey with the last tin of cat-food in the cupboard, unpack, stick the washing machine on and then redress before I head off to the supermarket in the next town, there being no food in the flat and I really need to stock up.

It's bloody freezing outside but I don't care, I still wear whatever I want - a white stretch-shirt (open low of course!) from H&M, a grey rib pencil-skirt from ASOS that is super-tight, a pair of grey suede ankle-boots from Bertie and the studded white leather biker jacket that Steve bought me for Christmas that I know for a fact cost him over £700! I also wear that open so everyone can see my beautiful full breasts. Underneath I'm wearing a matching bra and knickers in white from Curvy Kate as it's so cold I don't want my lips to stick together! Perfume is once again *Mademoiselle* by Chanel whilst my make-up is done to its usual impeccable high standard, making me look drop-dead gorgeous. I grab my keys and purse and then hit the shops.

The supermarket is packed but I find a parking space quick enough so as not to make me swear like usual. Inside though it's even worse and I'm immediately confronted by a short horrible obese girl with a big fat arse and legs pushing her screaming kid along in a buggy, some dim-looking Council-type bitch. I must be at least a foot taller than her! What a delicate flower she must be? The noise from her brat drives me insane and I just want to strangle it, and the mother too when I walk past it and notice the kid is a disgusting dysgenic mixture of black and white.

A dark cloud of infanticide looms over me, she's actually proud of her mongrel! I throw the mother a glare but she's too thick to understand me although she senses my aura; my persona, my style, my height, my pace, my money, legs, shoes, hair, face, breasts, everything. She's jealous and so she fucking should be - ugly slag! My eyes should not be subjected to scum like her. I'm in no doubt whatsoever that she's sponging off the State using my hard-earned tax money. Why is it that wherever I go or whatever I do, I've always got some fucker in my face?

I change gear and head for the vegetable section and then on and around the store at my usual high-speed and precision. I take a quick look around the clothes isles but there's nothing I want. In all I've collected approximately twenty items and so make my way to the till.

There's an old couple in front of me in the queue, both in their eighties by the looks of them. The wife is quite sweet-looking and smiles at me as I place my things onto the conveyor-belt but the husband is a bit of a weirdo and stares at me with a blank expression that gives me the creeps. I ignore the old tosser and look around me but all the while I detect him staring at my bare legs, my bum, my face and down my cleavage. I pick a magazine out from the small rack on the other side of the conveyor and flick through it in an attempt to distract myself. I can't believe they can charge almost 6-quid for some magazine about the local county that has half of it given over to posh adverts only the well-off can afford, hence the price of the mag I guess?

The guy on the checkout is around sixtyish and looks like a college professor - maybe he was? He obviously knows the old couple in front of me to some degree as I stand there waiting like a bloody lemon listening to their endless chat about nothing. Don't these old people realise that there's a queue behind them and they aren't the only customers in the World?

Finally they trundle off and I move up to the "professor". We exchange "Hellos" as he scans my goods across the scanner with a bleep whilst simultaneously scanning my breasts. I load my bags, pay, receipt, goodbye, out the door. Weirdo!

***

That afternoon I chill-out to some music - Bowie - and have a little white wine and some vodka, and turn my computer on to check my Emails. I only have a handful from the past few days as I quit the dating agency a month before Christmas as I'd totally lost interest in it. I found it far too dodgy - so many losers. My messages include two from Mum, one from Kate, one from Rachael at work and one from Steve with the body which I read first.

He hopes I had a nice Christmas at my Mum's and wonders what I'm doing? "Not much. I want to see you." I message him back and my blood pressure tightens, I can feel it, as I sit there thinking about him and what I want him to do to me. He's also has quit the agency - so he says? - and wants to meet up but can't make it either tonight or tomorrow due to family commitments, so how about Friday? I tell him Friday's okay and my heart explodes. I really do think about him a lot, he's a great guy but I could never truly fall in love with him, I just don't want to. How could I ever trust him? How can I trust any man? I think I've forgotten how to love, the delirious drug that it is.

I put a quarter measure of vodka in my wine glass and fill the remainder up with wine and down it all in one gulp. The third glass goes down just as easy and I strip off all my clothes and masturbate using 2-wine / vodka soaked fingers in my slit as I think about what Steve is going to do to me and I cum down my legs in under a minute. My breathing and my body become spasticated as I wank myself and cum again and lick my own juice from my fingers.

Thursday is spent catching up on essentials around the flat and other stuff; washing, drying, ironing, vacuuming, computer, Emails, depilating, vodka, showering, cooking, lager, washing up, Lacey, phone, wine, TV, bed. I dream of Steve that night, of getting married, buying a house, a mortgage, having kids, arguments, divorcing, nightmares, blood, death, ghosts, phantoms, vampires.

***

This morning I'm up like a lark as to what I'm about to receive. The bubbles of anticipation burst throughout my body; I want him to take me to heaven and leave me there for a thousand years as he pampers me and feeds my pangs of carnal delight.

It being Friday, I'm going to ask Steve to stay the night. I didn't ask him in my Emails just in case he said "No" and then I would've dwelt on my grief. This way if he turns me down then I'll have less time to think about being let down. Does that make sense? I think it does anyway? I know how to play with the minds of men just as well as their bodies.

Anyway, Steve's not due here until mid-day so I spend the morning doing my hair, make-up and nails, all after a nice long soak in the bath where I clean myself thoroughly inside and out. When I think I'm finished I check-out my reflection in the mirror and I'm more than proud of the result - I look fucking gorgeous, way good enough for any man, way good enough to give any top model a scare.

I laugh out loud at myself for being me and pour myself a large vodka to celebrate, the time now being 11.15am. I preen and dance about the flat naked as Lacey looks at me like I'm completely bloody stupid even though she's seen me do this a thousand times before. Life is a drug to me that I feed like a fetish.

The door-bell rings at 11.35am. That can't be him already can it? I rush to the window to check the visitor's car park and see Steve's car sitting there in one of the bays. My heart jumps out of my chest as I run to the front door, wrenching it open without a single care in the World, much to Steve's surprise as I'm still completely naked, I just don't fucking care!

Before he even has a chance to complete the word "Wow" I jump on him, wrapping my arms around him and kissing him hard and full-on. I want him now. I want him inside me. I want him to love me.

I reach down between his legs and rub his cock and feel it rapidly grow against my touch. I slide down onto my knees and rub him harder but he warns me off:

"Sarah, the bloody door's still open girl! Come on, it's freezing outside, people will see you."

"I don't give a shit, I want you." I fire back at him.

He grabs my wrists laughing and shuffles us both inside, shutting the door behind him with his foot.

"Look at you; you're like a bitch on heat!"

"I can't help it, I need you, come on." I reply, grinning like a cat.

"And I want you babe, but at least let me get my clothes off and then you can do whatever you like."

"You know what I like and I want it all." I say to him like a dirty bitch.

He takes his jacket off and throws it on the floor. We kiss again and he squeezes one of my breasts and starts to finger my vagina. I force my hand down his jeans and fondle his cock inside his pants and he's already hard and hot. I squat down on my haunches and drop his clothes to the floor with his member springing out at me ready for action, its thick veiny shaft and bulging shinny purple knob staring me in the face.

I swallow him whole and he gasps for air and moans as I suck him hard and wank myself with 2-fingers and I cum. I use my own honey on him as I un-suck and wank him off as I tug on his sack.

I sense something wonderful is about to happen - he cums in my face.

He screams as he cums at me, spurting his muck over my face and tits and I love him and suck and lick it, forming rivulets of milky cum that run out from the corners of my mouth.

I go and wash off Steve's mess and return to find him naked on the sofa, still hard and ready for my body. We laugh and small-talk as I climb on top of him and rubber his cock and then lube myself with my index finger.

We both smile at each other as I near myself closer to him and take his cock in my right-hand and then sit on it, pressing his bulb between my bum-cheeks. Gently I lower myself down on him, forcing him into me and it stings and I cry in pain and pleasure. My cheeks part as he enters and I feel my insides move to accommodate him as he fucks my rear. We both moan deeply as he shafts my rectum, screwing each other in perfect synchro. His cock feels so good in me that I feel like I'm floating on cloud number-9!

After riding him for a while I partially climb off him and Steve's cock slides out of me with a squelch. I remove the rubber and wank him for a moment and then straddle him once more, inserting his bare tool into my vagina. I have to trust him as I have to trust myself otherwise the whole World will stop. My internal muscles are forced apart as he penetrates me fully and I squeeze him simultaneously with my arms and my vagina, gripping him tightly as he loves me.

The sheer bliss of his naked shaft throbs away inside my body as we fuck each other for what seems like forever until his body tightens and he grips my svelte body, screaming at me that he's about to cum.

"Cum in me babe, cum in me, it's okay, come on, fuck me, cum in me now, come on, fuck it." I shout at him as he fucks.

You always make me cum. I'll take it up the bum. Then you can lick my hole again.

He shoots up inside me and I catch the sensation of his seed filling my box, spitting his jet of life into my body. Together we're in rapture and I lean forward to kiss his chest. I stop my grinding and he touches my tits and squeezes my nipples and it literally feels like I'm sitting on a rock as his spent shaft stays firmly inside me.

I climb off him and collapse backwards with his thick cum oozing from my swollen vulva, my heavy spunk-laden labia hanging outside of me, throbbing with pain and heat. He reaches out to me and touches my creampie with his fingers, making me shake uncontrollably and I want to cum again but I can't.

I feel like I've been to Hell and back. I want him to need me. I want him to love me. I reach out with my left-hand and wank him slowly and gently as I touch my raw meat with my other and it feels so good that I sigh in pure pleasure.

Both completely expended I bend over to him and tenderly kiss his knob. We move closer and kiss like lovers and embrace, lying rectilinear with each other wrapped in each other's arms. He must want me, mustn't he? He has to? How can he not love me when I'm in love with myself so much? I am beautiful to both men and women so where's the problem? There is none. I am the Queen of all Queens.

Steve and I spend the rest of the day, and all day Saturday as well as he wanted to stay over in the end - much to my joy! - doing all the things that couples do. We have sex; we eat, watch TV, kiss, cuddle, go shopping, have a walk in the local park, have a laugh, drink and just be together like lovers.

Tonight though, the two of us are going out to dinner at an English restaurant in Kingswood, buried in the heart of deepest Surrey that Steve knows and has got us a reservation there at 7.30pm. I'm going for my hyper-model look tonight featuring my full-on war-paint make-up that includes cherry-coloured lipstick, coal-black eye-shadow and my hair up and immaculate as ever.

As for my clothes - or lack of them depending on which way you look at it! - I'm wearing a tight little black Rebel dress from BB Dakota that has a huge plunging neckline that exposes most of my tits. Its a dress that every girl should have at least one of - that is of course if you've got a body like mine to go inside it! On my feet I'm wearing a pair of crazy stiletto-heeled platform court shoes in black from Polyvore. My clutch-bag tonight is a white and black Molly cutwork one from BooHoo. I must also add that I'm not wearing any underwear because I don't want to. My perfume tonight is *Mademoiselle* by Chanel once again.

Steve drives tonight and we arrive at our destination at 7.10pm and settle ourselves down in the corner of the bar for a quick drink first, both of us having a lager each. The restaurant itself is reasonably busy, just as you would expect at this time of the day and for this affluent area. We make our way to our table and order. Our waitress is a young girl in her early-20's, slim and blonde with a nice tight figure, but in no way am I jealous. Looking the way I do tonight there is no-one on this Earth that looks more stunning than I do right now - so fucking there!

However, no sooner does the waitress open her mouth do I understand what I'm dealing with once again - she's yet another bloody Slav! Either bloody Polish, Bulgarian or Romanian it doesn't matter, they're all the fucking same. I really shouldn't be amazed but I am this time and I let out a deep sigh of exasperation which fortunately Steve doesn't pick up on. If I go to a French restaurant I'm served by someone French, likewise the same with Italian / Italian, Chinese / Chinese and so on. So why is it every time I go somewhere supposedly English I'm confronted by a bloody foreigner, usually a fucking Slav? She's a nice enough girl but that's not the bloody point - where have all the sodding English people gone?

We order a bottle of wine between us - German white of course! - and for our meals I order a steak (rare) with chips, peas and a side-salad whilst Steve orders Haddock in white sauce, new potatoes, broccoli and carrots. The food is glorious as is the wine - a really expensive bottle that costs over £20! - and we eat, drink and enjoy each other's company. I am so happy that I can't stop giggling like a big soppy tart!

For desert we have Christmas pudding with ice cream and brandy butter and it all tastes absolutely yum. We follow with a Latte each, all of which is expertly made and beautifully presented. The Polish girl brings us the bill and Steve pays just as a gentleman should, giving a small tip for the waitress. I'd also like to give her a tip - fuck off back to fucking Poland where you fucking belong you fucking Slav bitch!

With my doggy-bag (or should that be catty-bag?) in hand for Lacey containing a few pieces of steak as well as some fatty bits from around the edge, we head off to the car park where we kiss and make-out up against the side of Steve's car with lots of touching and caressing.

Another couple walk by giggling and pointing at us but we ignore them and carry on regardless. Steve puts his hand up my dress and touches my vagina and I moan out loud as I spasm uncontrollably.

* * *

Saturday came and went all too soon; Steve had to leave after lunch-time and after sex as he was flying out to America for a business meeting and other stuff early Sunday morning for the company he works for. He won't be back in England for another three whole weeks!

What am I going to do with myself? I love him for being part of my life but now he's gone. To say that I'm sad and depressed doesn't even come close to the truth.

I miss him so much already and it's only bloody Sunday morning! I've given myself too him totally - my mind, my body, my soul, my complete existence. I really do think I love him. I am scared but I'm lonely. Lacey and alcohol keep me going but it's just not enough. It's not the answer to the problem.

But do I really love him? I think I do but I'm just not sure? I haven't actually said the L-word too him yet and he hasn't said it to me either so I don't really know where I stand. Love brings happiness but it also brings heartache.

If he's just using me or has another girl in tow or is lying to me then I'll kill myself of that I'm absolutely certain. I will poison Lacey and then slash my wrists.

How can I think of such horrible things? I should be happy and I really want to be so why can't I just do it? I start to think of "Him", the ex I can't even bare to mention and then of my so-called "Father" and all the fucking horror that he put me through in my younger days, including how he treated Mum and my sister Kate.

I know on the outside that I'm beautiful, calm, sure, poised, strong and positive, but on the inside I am rotten to the core and cut to ribbons. What will it take to tie all those pieces back together? Who is capable of doing that? Am I? Steve? Someone else? I really don't know.

My life has been nothing but a series of disappointments, loosely stitched together with occasional glimmers of hope and forced pleasures.

Just thinking about the whole situation starts to wind me up and I cry and drink. I hate being damaged and I cry and drink some more and life just isn't fair.

It just isn't fucking fair.

15

I Want

Well now. Things have finally, after months of speculation and stupid rumours flying about, come to a conclusion at work. That being that my bitch of a supervisor Inga has finally decided to retire at long bloody last. Why on Earth she left it this late is beyond anyone's guess? And why do it straight after Christmas? Surely do it beforehand would have been the normal thing to do? Talk about unprofessional.

There is still one rumour flying around though, that is to who's going to take over from her? The main candidate being yours truly the wonderfully gorgeous me! As I've already told you before though, I don't want the bloody job; in fact I don't really want any fucking job thank you! I just don't need the hassle. Yes, I know the extra money would be nice but at the end of the day I don't want to be a pawn in someone else's game; I'm a sycophant to no-one. I am a free-spirit that cannot be caged and I'm not going to waste my life doing things that other people want me to do.

You might be sitting there thinking that I do that anyway, and you would be right, but with the added pressure that would be put upon me by running this department do you honestly think I'll be better off mentally? No I wouldn't. As I say, financially it would be a different story, but money in the bank is not the be-all-and-end-all to life or even being alive itself for that matter. Freedom from all the bullshit in this World and having my own piece of mind is far more important to me.

The decision not to take the supervisors job was an easy one, born from seeking guidance from my inner spiritual self.

If you don't have faith in yourself then you have nothing. If there's one thing that's worse than being let down by others then that's letting yourself down. I have to focus on my will to succeed; for myself and no-one else.

Anyway, the upshot of my decision will be finalised this morning as I've been called into a meeting with my department manager Mr. Wingate, or "Wingnut" as I've nicknamed him because of his sticky-out ears! He's a funny senile old bugger - I guess he's in his mid-to-late-60's - with a very large chip on his shoulder, as all managers have. Today though I intend to knock that chip off, or at least reduce it in size somewhat by telling him that I'm not interested in the promotion.

I don't know why it is that everyone has to pussy-foot around the boss like he's some sort-of fucking Demi-God? He's a human being just the same as everyone else, even me - well, maybe not quite the same as me but you know what I mean? - so why does everyone treat him like he's so bloody superior?

These fake managers with their pseudo-bullying attitudes are nothing. I am real, they are not. The bullies of the World are the losers, for they have no feeling of life.

I'm wearing my full-on power make-up today, coupled with an extremely short white bodycon mini-skirt from Misguided, a white Oxford waistcoat over a light-blue blouse from H&M that's bursting at the buttons exposing my full cleavage, and my fave pair of blue-suede Lola platform court shoes. My perfume is *Mademoiselle* by Chanel. If the sight of that little lot as well as my beautiful long toned legs doesn't get him all hot and flustered then nothing will! Poor old shite-boss!

It's 10am exactly when I knock on the already open door to "Wingnuts" office. He looks at me and stares at my body like it's the first time he's ever seen a woman, or at least one as gorgeous as me anyway! After a short exchange of the usual pleasantries I sit my bum down in front of him with my long legs crossed provocatively so he can get the full effect of what I've been blessed with.

I give it to him straight with no beating around the bush or letting him mess around with me. I inform him of my decision that "I'm not interested in the supervisor's position" and he just sits there looking at me like I've kicked him in the balls, stunned into silence.

After some 15-minutes of banter between us as to the whys-and-wherefores of my decision - along with plenty of leg and breast gorping on his part! - I stand to leave, springing to my feet like a Spring flower. I exit and make my way back to my desk, leaving "Wingnut" slumped back in his chair like I've just stick a knife in his throat - condescending old bastard!

Back in my department office I give Rachael a quick nod and a smile as I pass her desk. She's the only one here I've told about turning the job down and I've trusted her with keeping quiet, which she has. As I sit back down at my position I feel a thousand eyes upon me as I put my headset on and take a customer's call. I can tell that my fellow co-workers are just dying to know if I'm going to be their new boss; their expressions are so bloody obvious it's a joke.

I look around at all these people surrounding me as I type my next customer's details into my computer; they are nothing but sheep and just about as intelligent. They have absolutely no idea of what I'm about, absolutely no concept at all. They will never understand the reasons for my existence let alone why I turned the job down. They have no inkling at all as to my life and its successes and failures. My future success will be my own for me to enjoy and has nothing to do with them or anyone else. The best and worst of me is still yet still to come.

Life is but a paradox, an absurd self-conflicting element that one has to battle with and against every bloody day just in order to exist. My whole life is a fight - a fight to get up, a fight to get to work, a fight at work, a fight to get back home again, a fight to stay sane and a fight to stay alive.

Time is chasing all of us and one day we will all be caught. The falling sands of time wait for no-one.

The onus is on myself to try and continue and see my existence through to the bitter end, whatever that may be? I try to conceptualize my future through my will in order to keep fighting on. If anyone thinks that refusing this promotion or to continue working here in this ridiculous job with these cretins is what I actually exist for in life then they too are as mad as each other.

Do you understand how much I love my life? Or exactly how much I love being alive? I don't think you or anyone can. I am above you all in the clouds. I know how to bend the curve of life itself and nothing and no-one can touch me. I know I'm not perfect - except in looks of course! - what with the drinking and all the other stuff, maybe even my mental state is also questionable to some degree, but that's not the point.

I don't need anyone to tell me that I'm wrong. With age, experience and the passing of time I have become self-diagnostic. I know what I am and what I want. That's the way it is, take it or leave it.

***

The day has gone amazingly quickly really for some reason? Probably due to my state of mind at the moment or the fact that we have plenty of work in the office, who knows? Anyway, I'm off to the supermarket on the way home just to get a few odds and ends, nothing specific.

As is the norm over the past couple of months or so, the traffic is bloody terrible around near the supermarket, with road-works everywhere. An article in my local paper said it's something to do with laying cables or some such shit? Anyway it's taken me at least 20-minutes extra just to get here never mind getting through the sodding entrance gate!

All this crap just strengthens my resolve to move further South. I'll just have to wait and see if the congestion improves when the work is finished or not? Just like everything else, what happens in the present shapes our future lives, no matter what.

Once through the gate I park surprisingly easily and make my way to the large sliding automatic entrance doors. Before me I immediately spy yet more detritus - the depressing and dirty (literally) figures of a group of scrounging bloody Romanian scum that I can't even bring myself to call human. To say they're like animals would be disrespectful to animals. They have no respect for themselves let alone anyone else.

With them are four horrible kids that look like rats, all begging for money from passersby. The "Mother", a short fat dirty lump, is dressed in some sort-of Gypsy garb that when I get closer to her I actually notice she's probably the same bloody age as me but looks more like eighty! Next to her stands who I presume is her so-called "Husband", a skinny little runt of a "person" dressed all in black who looks straight into my eyes and grins a fake grin at me thus exposing a mouthful of broken tobacco-stained rotten teeth that sends a shiver down my spine.

I want to shoot all six of them dead right here and now but I have no weapon to hand other than my total and complete disgust. It isn't just my disgust though for having to view them, but also for the fact that not only are they here in my Country but the fucking Government lets them in in the first fucking place and then considers them to be an "asset" to our economy and our nation's future? It is complete fucking madness. They should all be fucking exterminated.

The supermarket is reasonably busy inside but not excessively so. I grab a basket and wander around looking for things to buy but I don't come away with much, just the usual - cat food, chocolate, crisps, a nice piece of rib-eye and a bottle of German white wine - all for tonight. Not the cat food though, that would be disgusting!

I stand at the till flanked by people, just people, nothing more or less. They all look at me in the same way as everyone else does, checking out my body - my breasts, legs, bum, hair, make-up, mouth etc. etc. The men look at what they want but can't have while the women look at what they dream to look like but know that it's futile to even think of attaining my level as it will never happen in a million-years. I understand my looks can be quite intimidating to most women but what do they expect me to do about it? It's their bloody problem, not mine!

The young guy on the checkout looks about 19 or 20 at a guess. He looks at my breasts and then my face and smiles so I give him one of my knowing smiles back. As he passes my items over the scanner with a beep he changes his position from sitting to standing - it's wildly obvious as to why? Just so he can get a closer look down my cleavage - cheeky little sod! Even so I like it and it starts to make my heart beat faster which in turn makes my breasts heave and more enticing.

My bill comes to just over 25-quid which I pay on my debit card as I don't have or believe in credit cards or any of that shit. I insert my card in the slot in the machine and bend forward to key-in my pin-number, purposely exposing more of my firm peaches for the young guy to see. I suddenly and quickly look up and catch him doing just that but he doesn't look away, just cheekily continues to stare at my mounds!

Once accepted I remove my card and slot it back into my purse, a crystal-silver metal one from Dbase. Similarly at the same time I remove one of my private hand-written cards that features just my first name and Email address. Gary - the young guy's name that I notice from the badge on his shirt - looks a little taken-aback as I hand it to him in exchange as he hands me my receipt. He stands there totally perplexed as to either what to say or do as I continue to load-up my bag of goodies and make my exit. The poor lad holds out his hand to return my card back to me but I decline it with a small shake of my head. He simply hasn't a clue which way to turn as I smile back at him and walk off in my own special and unique way, leaving him standing there open-mouthed as I tell him softly to: "Email me."

I feel somewhat pleased with myself as I sit myself back in the car; the power I exert over any man I want is amazing and is really quite awesome. It's almost spiritually uplifting!

I sit there smiling to myself for a moment as a young couple, both around my age by the looks of them, and their baby - I can't tell if its a boy or a girl - are arguing with each other as they load up their car that's parked next to mine. As I reverse out of my space and head for home, both parents stare at me as I drive away. Why are they staring? Are they remembering their lost freedom and independence before the kid came along or what I wonder to myself? I hope so and I'm glad that they're jealous of me and I'm happy to watch them squirm. Why do people have kids and then all they do is bloody moan about them? In that case why have them in the first bloody place? Are they really that bloody stupid?

A couple and their child. And me. And me and who? And me and what?

It's 6.30pm by the time I walk through my front door and I'm greeted as ever by Lacey who always somehow seems to detect that I've got cat food with me? I kick my shoes off in the hallway and head for the kitchen to unload my shopping and feed Lacey as she purrs around me like a thing possessed, drunk on love. I put the wine in the freezer to chill quicker than it would do in the fridge as I then prepare dinner for myself; the lovely piece of steak I just bought along with fried onions, chips and some mixed salad.

In the living room I click the TV on as I wait for the chips and onions to fry and catch today's news report. Unbelievably yet another bastard politician has been caught with his fingers in the till! Who the fuck do these people think they are going around ripping-off their own Country? Don't they realize that it's they who should be setting an example for the people to follow? They're all fucking morons, the lot of them!

In today's modern society virtually anything goes, with the rot starting at the top and filtering down. The stupid Government and its stupid politicians do exactly what they like without a bloody care in the World for anyone in it so why the fuck should I or anyone else? I'm going to continue living my life according to me and no-one else and that's the be-all-and-end-all of it.

I understand that if everyone felt and did as they pleased then society as a whole would come crashing down, I'm not that stupid or naive to recognize the failings of my statement but that's the way it is for me at this juncture of my life. Maybe when I hit forty or whenever then things will be different, who knows? They probably won't! Maybe by then I will have found a nice guy and would have settled down - dread the thought! Seriously though, if things carry on the way they are for the next 20-years or so down this slippery slope then where will it all end?

I leave the TV to itself as I finish cooking my dinner, frying the steak medium-rare and fixing the side-salad. After I've already sunk a couple of glasses of wine in the kitchen I finally sit my bum down with my meal in front of the box. I've given up on the news as it's far too depressing so I find a home-finding show on another channel featuring a couple of lesbians that are looking for a holiday home in Spain. The one they eventually settle for is in the middle of bloody nowhere, a dust-bowl area of land that looks like the surface of the Moon and is just about as inviting! I'd be bored out of my bloody skull living there!

The steak is spot-on and slides down beautifully, as does the wine, which by now is nearly all finished and I'm feeling a little piddly! I switch the TV off as I've had quite enough of all that crap for now and dump my empty plate in the kitchen sink, have a quick wee, and then turn my computer on to catch up on my Emails.

Once again it's the usual old stuff - Mum complaining about the bloody neighbours, Kate going on about having no money and the baby continuously crying, several messages from Steve who is still in the US saying how much he misses me blah blah blah and all that crap. If he really misses me that much then how come I haven't seen him for nearly 3-bloody-months then? Answer that one? I know he's busy in the States with his work and all that stuff, but 3-months - really?

I wade through my messages, deleting them as I go, the majority of them being from companies flogging so-called super-saving deals on their crap products but I'm really not interested in any of that shit. It's the last message on my list that catches my attention, even though I'm a bit numbed from the wine, the whole bottle now empty. It's from Gary, the young guy from the supermarket checkout earlier, asking me: "How are you?" and "What do you do for a living?" and "Where do you live?" and "Are you married?" and "Do you have any kids?" and on and on and on and all that old crap.

I feel rather superior that he's contacted me so soon and I immediately start to feel all hot and horny inside. I message him back with all the answers to his myriad of questions, ending my message with an offer of a drink sometime?

You should by now understand some of the reasons for me being the way I am?

In 2-shakes of a lamb's tail he replies, saying: "I already have a girlfriend but I would still like to meet you for a drink if you want?"

Well, so much for his poor girlfriend then! I'm guessing to myself that there's no-way on this Earth that she can be better looking than me, she's probably just some inexperienced kid, as is he. Anyway, with plenty of cheek on my part I decide to invite him here to my place tonight at 9pm for that drink. How can he possibly refuse?

It takes him a mere split-second to answer me back with a "Yes" and that: "I have to get the bus to your place because I haven't passed my driving test yet." Ah, bless!

I strip naked and jump in the shower for a quick one, desperately trying to avoid getting my hair wet or ruining my make-up as they're both still pretty-much perfect from this morning, only needing a light touch-up. I'm also still really smooth so there's no need to worry about that either. I gently dry myself off by patting my lovely silky skin with one of my white Egyptian towels and then retouch my make-up and tidy my hair just a little by retying it back up in its usual pony-tail using a black satin bow. I add a few squirts of perfume - *Opium* by Yves Saint Laurent - no overkill though, and then I'm pretty much done and dusted.

I put on my black Japanese silk Kimono babydoll dressing gown from Kouichi - nothing else - and pour myself a large neat vodka. Lacey looks at me with those big yellow eyes of hers. What a clever girl she is, she already knows how this evening is going to progress - bless her - as she's seen this scenario played out a hundred times or more.

I pose on my balcony like the Princess I am, viewing my people, my town and my Country. I can see everyone down below but no-one can see me as I am invisible to the whole fucking World.

My door-bell chimes at 8.50pm and he's early - good boy! Lacey stands to attention and her ears prick up as I make my way to the front door, putting my drink down on the glass coffee table as I go. Taking a deep breath for bravery I open it and suddenly we stand facing one another once again.

"Hi, I've got the right flat then?" He says, looking a little older and somewhat different in his own clothes than I remember from earlier.

"You found it okay?" I come back, although I don't want to continue with this stupid small-talk for much longer, not on the door step anyway.

"Yes, I came straight here really."

"Well good. Come here then." I say as I grab his arm with one hand and the back of his neck with the other and pull him towards me, kissing him hard on the lips with the passion of lovers. He returns my kiss, albeit with some surprise, as I manoeuvre him into my flat - my lair - and kick the door shut with my right-foot.

We embrace hard and I begin flicking my tongue in and out of his young mouth as I move my left-hand down to between his legs. I touch his stiffening cock and I sense it growing with my rough touch. He gasps as I stroke him for a while, although momentarily I let him go as I pull at the belt of my gown and let it glide its shinny silkiness down my perfect smooth skin and crumple to the floor.

Without any encouragement he places one hand on one of my pert bum-cheeks and the other on one of my firm breasts, squeezing and caressing each with his lust. Suddenly he stops mid-kiss and starts to bleat at me, just like a sheep:

"I shouldn't be doing this. I already have a girlfriend."

"Then why did you come here?" I softly but firmly quiz him.

"I don't know. I think you're beautiful, like a Goddess." He exclaims, as if I didn't know that already!

I smirk at his statement and lick my lips slowly and drop down onto my knees. He sighs as I touch his bulge and start to undo his jeans. I rub him again through the thinner layer of his boxer-shorts and I feel his length in my hand, a good 5 to 6-inches and hot. I play around with his shaft behind the material and then pull them down his legs to reveal his stiff penis, it springing out to greet me with all its love.

Using both hands I wank him with one and massage his balls with the other, making him cry with pleasure. Moving closer to him I kiss his knob and he loses control and starts to shake and quiver all over. I tongue at him, tasting the saltiness of his throbbing skin and his tight balls as I then take him fully into my mouth. I suck hard on his cock as I squeeze and yank gently on his nuts and he starts to pant heavily as I bring him to his height, running my teeth over his shaft.

He can contain himself no longer and spurts his spunk straight to the back of my mouth, his muck hitting my uvula and sliding down my windpipe, making me cough. I continue to suck and lick him even though he's now expended his milky load into me, running my cum-coated mouth and tongue over his cock and balls to both our joy.

I stand and leave him to recover as I make my naked way to the bathroom to spit and clean up, all in total silence as there are no need for words. Upon my return I find Gary in the living room fixing himself a vodka - I don't have any other spirits apart from gin - which he then downs almost all of it in one big gulp. I position myself behind him and wrap my arms around his body and begin to rub my vagina against his bum. He turns around and laughs at my action and we kiss softly as I start once more to rub his dick to hardness, he in turn fingering my box and I love it.

I have this young guy in my flat and I'm naked with his fingers inside my body and I want him all. I'm such a lucky fucking bitch!

"I can't believe this is happening to me." He tells me.

"Well it's true. I will do anything you want me to do. Tonight is your night as well as mine. I want you to fuck me." I whisper to him seductively.

I order him to remove all his clothes as I fix myself a large vodka and he undresses before me. Some idle chit-chat between us reveals that he's not 19 or 20 as I first thought but that he's only 18-years old! How fucking cheeky am I? I really don't fucking care how old he is, as long as he can keep it up and give me a good fuck then I don't give a shit, that will be good enough for me right now.

I watch him become naked in front of my eyes and I rub my breasts and finger myself as he does so. He doesn't have the greatest body in the World, not like Steve's, but that's not the point. He's my fuck-buddy for tonight and that's all I need and want.

I giggle at his nakedness, not in a piss-taking way, but in a cheeky girly manner. His young body makes me feel like some kind-of cougar but I'm too young to be one of those. I stand before him and wank him back to attention as he fondles my breasts. I turn my back on him and lean over the arm of the sofa and spread my beautiful legs apart, signalling him to take me from behind. I don't bother with using a rubber, I know that I'm clean and at only 18 I put my faith and trust in him that he is also.

Gary moves into position behind me, placing his hands on either side of my pelvis to grab hold and then I feel him, his young meat inserting itself into my wet pie. He starts pounding-away at me, the energy of his young body ramming into my hole and I want it all and forever until suddenly I begin to shake as I cum over him and down my legs my special honey of love. Before long he cums into me, glopping his seed inside and we scream in unison of our naked beings.

He slithers out of my vagina and I turn to kiss his mouth in gratitude for spunking me. Lowering myself down on my haunches I lick at his cum and vaginal fluid-covered dick, kissing it, drinking it, eating it. He winces as I suck him dry, his chest beating out of time as I begin to wank myself with 2-fingers in and out of my cunt.

I cum. I am happy. I am at total peace with the World and everything is rosy. I try to stand but my legs are drained of power and I stumble into his arms and we laugh.

"Are you real or just a dream?" He says to me, catching me unawares.

"What do you mean?" I reply quizzically.

"I can't believe this is happening. You're amazing. You're so beautiful." He returns.

"I know I am, there's no need to tell me. Come on, I want you again." I order him.

I drop down on one knee and as I finger my twat he fucks my mouth like he did my vagina. I don't suck him; I just let him slide his cock in and out of my face. He's hard but he's all spent as I think I may have pushed him too far too soon and drained him. I let him ride my tongue for a while longer as then I insert a wet finger into his bum, immediately causing him to momentarily lose his rhythm. Suddenly from nowhere he cums onto my tongue, just a small amount, and I kiss his shinning knob - Ha!

We both go and shower together and the hot water bouncing on our nakedness is so beautiful. I ask him about his girlfriend but he's a little reluctant to answer me or commit himself. He's probably embarrassed for cheating on her I surmise?

We dry each other's skin and I then make coffee for us both in the kitchen, also giving Lacey her nightly feed while I'm there. The conversation is a little strained now for some reason, maybe due to the age gap between us or the fact that both of us are still completely naked? I suspect that he's greatly in awe of my perfect body and in his eyes I must seem somewhat unreal?

He then shows me some photos of his girlfriend - Sam - on his phone and I'm a bit surprised to see that she's actually very pretty - tall, slim and with a nice figure and only 17. As he shows me her pictures I kiss him on the cheek and then I drop to my knees and start to play with his cock and balls with my tongue, licking him all over his stiffening shaft and tight sack. He almost drops his coffee on my head as I suck him hard, his purple-helmet swelling up inside my mouth but before long I let him go.

I then lead him into the living room and lay him down on my white shaggy rug on the floor, positioning myself over him and straddling his face. Turning away from his body I widen my legs apart and lower myself down onto him.

"Lick my cunt and fuck me with your tongue" I order him.

I feel him work his way between my lips with his tongue, the sensation launching me into outer-space with the thrill and emotion of his touch. I can't control myself and I cum over his face as I fondle my tits and I shudder and I cum and spit.

"I love your vagina." He splutters to me from below.

"So do I. Lick me" I counter breathlessly.

He laps at my clit until I can take no more. I think I'm about to have a heart attack but I don't and I cum on him once again.

We're both completely knackered by now and I lay on top of his young body in an all-enveloping embrace as we kiss each other passionately, nothing else. The oily goo of my cum feels fantastic between our mouths as we snog and we're both in rapture and I want to remain in this position for the rest of my days on this Earth.

I am in love with him as he is with me.

We fool around with each other's naked bodies for a while longer before we go and clean ourselves up once more in the shower. He has to go home, back to the fold, back to his little girl Sam. She can have him back, I don't mind or care as I can have any man I want, whenever I want. I can have any woman either for that matter; if that's the way I want to go ever again? It is totally my choice in what I do and no-one is going to fucking stop me.

I always try to be honest, not necessarily with anyone else, but with myself. I am strong enough to walk through Hell with a smile on my face, my head held high and my dignity intact.

***

I slept like a log last night and this morning I'm on top of the World. It must have been all that extra protean I ingested last night!

Anyway, I'm up and about like a spring lamb although I suddenly notice that unusually Lacey isn't on my bed like she normally is when I awake and it makes me a little curious and somewhat concerned.

I make my way into the kitchen and click the kettle on, noticing that both Lacey's food and water bowls haven't been touched, something that has happened quite a few times recently.

In the living room I find her dozing on the sofa, sitting there with her front paws tucked-in under her body like all cats do. When I touch her though she doesn't move and an icy wave of fear and dread clouds over me as if Death himself has put his hand on my shoulder. I can see that she's still alive as the side of her body is still pulsating from her heartbeat, albeit slowly. I stroke her under her chin and she opens her big yellow eyes and looks up at me just like a sick animal does, with a wounded expression that makes my heart sink like a stone.

A soft kiss to the top of her head has no effect whatsoever and I begin to feel her pain creeping its way into my very soul

184

and I want to cry but I mustn't or I'll upset her even more. I kiss her once again still with no response and so go and fetch her a bowl of fresh food, one of her favourites of duck in sauce with garden vegetables, and place it on the floor in front of her. To my amazement she suddenly rises to her feet, stretching and arching her back just like a cat does. Horrifyingly though, as she does this she lets out a feint yelp that sends a cold shiver down my spine. She jumps off the sofa slowly with another small cry and starts to lick at her food. This is definitely not right. She's obviously in some kind-of pain.

Several times in her long life she's hurt herself by jumping down from things - the work surface in the kitchen, the sofa, the bed and in other ways - and I only hope and pray that is all it is again this time but in my heart of heart's I fear the worst. My poor baby. My Lace.

As she munches away on her food I desperately try to calm myself down, after all I still have to get ready for bloody work. I try and pull myself together but it's not easy, it being way too early for a large stiff vodka, although the tempting thought of having one does flash through my mind for a second.

I shower and get dressed in record time even though by now I'm already late. I keep my clothes nice and simple today with only light make-up, sexy white underwear from Ann Summers, a simple white blouse from Land's End, a black 1950's-style pencil-skirt from 20th Century Foxy and a pair of tan-coloured suede heels from Luichiny. My perfume today is *Luxe* by Avon.

I spend the day at work - same shit, different day - in a state of total oblivion to my surroundings as the tentacles of doom spread throughout my mind. I sometimes wonder if my life is some sort-of sick joke and that at any moment I'll wake up and actually find myself at peace for a bloody change? Fat chance!

I keep myself to myself for the entire day as I just sit there thinking about Lacey. I really hope that her pain is nothing serious and that she's only pulled a muscle as before.

At the end of yet another shitty day at work I race back home in near record speed and pull-up with squealing tyres in my parking space outside my flat. Once again fear washes over me as I wonder what I will find on the other side of my front door? I take a brave-pill and venture inside, calling out to my love as I always do but only silence comes the reply.

In the living room I find her in exactly the same place and position as I left her this morning, which must be a good sign mustn't it? I sit myself down beside her and stroke her head and at least she responds this time to my touch and lifts her head to look up at me, although in her eyes I can tell that it's one of help.

On the floor I notice that the bowl of her favourite food I left there this morning still has pretty-much the same amount in it as when I left the flat nearly 10-hours ago.

I continue to stroke her soft fur and notice a change in its texture, like it has a kind-of oily feel to it, something that she's never had before. I go to pick her up and place her on my lap, putting one hand underneath her body to support her frame. As I do though I touch something wet and my first thought is that she must have wet herself, my poor little love. It's only when I remove my hand and look at it I find that its covered in a sticky mess of thick congealed blood. I stare at it in pure horror and disbelief and I feel myself turn pale with shock - my poor baby Lace.

I want to scream out loud but I don't want to give her a bloody heart-attack, and so I cover my mouth with my other hand to silence myself. Oh fucking Hell!

I place her gently back on the sofa and then hurriedly make my way to the bathroom. I quickly look back at her as she sits there staring at me like death, following my every move. In desperation I scrub my hand as hard as I dare as I attempt to remove her blood, it flicking everywhere as I do so - on the tiled walls in front of me, on my clothes and on the floor also. I suddenly gaze up and look at myself in the mirror and I'm saddened by the expression on my face, on the woman that is looking back at me, a look of pain, desperation and loneliness.

After drying my hands I remove my soiled top, clean up the blood splashes everywhere and then redress - putting on a black Riza blouse from Full Circle - and head back to the living room to phone the vets. Lacey just sits there in the same position, not even attempting to lick herself clean of the blood as I would have expected.

I have to tear myself away from looking at her as I speak to the receptionist at the veterinary surgery. I explain the situation to her the best I can as I try to keep myself together with the girl telling me to: "Bring her in straight away."

After trying to clean Lacey up without making her (and therefore me) cry, the next thing to do is to try and get her in her transport basket - not without some difficulty - and then grab my things before we set off to the vets practice, itself a distance of only 4-miles away or so.

In all honesty, I have absolutely no idea how the Hell I make it here, the bloody car must have been on some kind-of autopilot as I have no recollection of driving here at all, nothing. Usually Lacey hates car journeys and wails and moans all the time, but this time I hear not a single sound from her, not even a feint cry.

I park the car directly outside the vets and carry Lacey in. Inside, the waiting area is completely empty, much to my surprise and delight, except for the receptionist behind her desk - a pretty young girl in her early-20's who I haven't seen before - and the vet herself - a really attractive Australian girl called Amanda. She appears to be somewhere in her late-20's and that I've actually met once before when I brought Lacey in for her yearly booster injection some 3-months ago.

She ushers us in straight away and I place the basket on the examination table, open its wire door and gently ease Lacey out of the box. I stroke her with all my love and care as I explain to Amanda what has happened as she examines her all over, she paying particular attention to Lacey's stomach area and hind-quarters.

After listening to her breathing and her heart for several minutes, she hits me with the news that I was dreading all along - Lacey has a lump in her stomach.

I try my hardest to retain my dignity but it's no good, I completely lose control and break down, bursting into a flood of tears. They're not just any old tears either, they're the uncontrollable sobbing ones of the saddest, most heartfelt and painful kind and I want to die.

I carry on crying as Amanda tells me that she would like to keep Lacey in at the surgery overnight in order to run some tests and keep a general eye on her. I desperately try to regain some control of myself, even just for Lacey's sake, as she sits there looking at me with those big round sad yellow eyes of hers, staring at me with a sense of knowing as to both her problem and her ultimate fate.

It's just no good and I lose it again - I can't help it. I want to destroy the whole World as we know it and start again from scratch without all the shitty people, without wars and hate, without pain and hunger but with peace and love and me and my cat living in happiness forever more.

Of course I agree with Amanda to let Lacey stay with her but I already know the outcome as does Lacey herself. I say a tearful "Goodbye" to my love as I stroke her softly and give her a little kiss to the top of her head, not knowing if I will ever see her alive again.

Once more I arrive at my destination - this time my flat - with autopilot guiding me yet again. In my private World behind my front door I smash myself to pieces on alcohol, the blood-soaked sofa a reminder - not that I fucking need one - of this cruel and vicious World. I vodka myself to death in a matter of minutes and shout and scream at the World and myself for being such a bastard and with my head in my hands I sit and cry.

I collapse to the floor in the living room in complete despair and rest the right-hand side cheek of my face down in Lacey's blood and cry yet more tears of impending loss into it. I sit back and wail in grief and using both hands I start to rub the sticky red mixture all over my face and neck but in doing so I lose my balance and fall backwards onto the rug with a thud, hitting my head on the floor and momentarily jolting my sorrow to one side. For a brief second or two it suddenly makes me see sense of my madness but once again it's of no use - I just cannot contain myself any longer and I start to retch, puking-up a nasty mixture of the remains of my lunch-time sandwich and the evil vodka.

I know I can't carry on like this as its just plain futile; I have to face the reality of the situation even though I don't want to. I struggle to the shower on all-fours and in tears and crawl in still full-clothed. The blast of cold water hitting my head and body strikes me like a bolt of lightning but instead of reviving me it just leaves me feeling like shit.

I'm not actually sure how long I was in the shower but I know I must of either dozed-off or passed-out as either way, the time when I awake has drifted past 9pm and I have to move. I extricate myself from my sodden pit and strip-off all my clothes and gaze at my naked body in the bathroom's full-length mirror. I stand there staring at myself and ask how can someone so beautiful be so fucked-up at the same time?

What have I done that is so fucking bad that it warrants all this misery in my life?

Usually at this point - as you very well know by now - I would probably end up playing with myself in any which way I was feeling at the time. But not now, not with my little girl all alone and frightened out of her mind in some horrible cage awaiting who knows what? I just can't lower myself to do it, the thought isn't even in my mind, it just wouldn't be right or even justifiable.

***

My night is spent in a total daze. I don't think I slept much at all with the constant thought of what today might bring? I toast two-slices of bread for breakfast but the very first bite just lodges in my throat like a knife. Even with a quick slurp of tea it just won't budge so in the end I don't bother with it and chuck it in the bin.

I've decided I'm not going into work today; they can all fuck off. Yesterday was bad enough and I know in my heart that today is going to be worse. I phone-in at 8.30am and speak to Judy, the newly-appointed supervisor, and tell her my woes. I didn't hear her reply as I wasn't listening and I don't fucking care anyway as I'm taking the day off regardless and that's all there is to it.

At 9am sharp I ring the vets to see what's happening? The girl on reception - not the same one as yesterday - informs me that Lacey had a quiet night and that she's okay and for me to ring back at 1pm this afternoon for an update. That's all very well for her to say, but what the Hell am I supposed to do in the bloody meantime; I've got 4-hours to kill?

I give Mum a quick ring and we both cry down the phone to each other as I tell her my news. I'm somewhat surprised by my weeping as I didn't think I had any more tears left in me after yesterday.

I mull around the flat as I try to keep my mind off the obvious subject, mainly cleaning-up like a bloody mad woman all the detritus from my bender, not to mention Lacey's dried blood-stains - my poor little girl. Exhausted, I fix myself a mug of nice strong coffee with plenty of sugar and sit back and try to relax a bit. I'm so bloody knackered after all the events of last night, as well as the cleaning, and before long the dreaded clock hits its allotted deadline.

The receptionist tells me to: "Come in straight away."

I race to the surgery as fast as I dare, surrounded by a total numb feeling. I have to wait a short while before I'm ushered in as someone else is being seen to, although for some reason I'm actually quite calm now as I sit there waiting patiently in the reception area. The examination room door suddenly opens and makes me jump, as a little old lady in her 80's with her little white Scottie dog on its lead trots out closely followed by Amanda. She smiles a smile at me and ushers me in. We exchange small pleasantries and then walk through to the rear of the building where the holding-cages are located.

I apologise to her for yesterday's tears but she immediately dismisses me by saying: "Don't worry about that." I guess she must see similar sights and worse every day of the week? There's absolutely no way I could ever do her job, it would be far too heart-breaking.

We suddenly stop at Lacey's cage and there she is - my little girl - actually looking a bit brighter and perkier today after the painkillers that Amanda has given her. I'm soon brought back down to Earth with a jolt though as Amanda explains too me what I already know - Lacey has a tumour in her stomach and considering its size, its position and her age, there is no hope of recovery.

Her words flow over me like a cold wind. They are meaningless too me now although I surprise myself at my self-control. Why am I being so calm? Why don't I just punch the vet in the mouth right here and now? It's no use of course, as I've already resigned myself to the inevitable outcome so there's no need or point in making another bloody scene like I did yesterday, or worse for that matter.

Lacey looks at me in the way she always does, with a sense of knowing exactly what I'm thinking; only this time I know what she's thinking - it is time. We stare at each other in love as I poke my fingers through the squares of the mesh cage door and she rubs her little wet nose over them, exchanging each other's scent.

Amanda explains that the painkillers should last for 2-days maximum, after that it just wouldn't be fair to prolong her suffering any more. I have to agree with her as this time I'm faced with no other choice.

She carries my little girl out of the cage, putting her back in her basket for the short painful trip home. I thank Amanda for what she's done for my love and tell her that I will see her tomorrow evening - it now being Thursday - for what will be the inevitable. Although neither of us actually say that, we both know what it really means. Lacey and I make our exit and head off, homeward bound.

Back at the flat and once indoors I open the door to Lacey's basket and out she wanders. It's incredible the effects the drugs have had on her, she seems just like she was months ago, happy as she can be and full of the joys of life! I had put her slow pace down to her age - she is almost twenty after all - but I mustn't blame myself, there's nothing anyone can do. That doesn't make it any easier of course; it's a sad fact of life that we all have to deal with death at some stage or another.

I'm certainly not going back to work tomorrow either that's for sure, they can all get stuffed again, so I'm going to take another day off. I have to and need to spend one last day with my baby. She's stood by my side through thick and thin for almost the last 20-years and I can't leave her on her own while I piss-off to bloody work for the day. I have to be side-by-side with her on the final adventure that is death, I owe her that much at least.

I kiss and cuddle her gently and she snuggles-up to my face, purring- away with her love. We spend the rest of the day together at all times with a quiet night in stuck in front of the telly watching crap. Incredibly I don't even touch the drink; I just don't seem interested in it today. It wouldn't be fair if I got pissed out of my head in front of my beautiful cat on her last day on Earth.

***

That night Lacey and I sleep a peaceful sleep together but I awake early with a start, I feel something is just not quite right. She's lying right next to me on the bed but when I look into her eyes it is the face of death that stares back at me, a cold empty glare of nothing that takes my breath away. I touch the soft fur on her head and stroke her but she has no will to respond to my touch. I place my other hand under her chin and raise her head but although she's still alive she is also dead. This is the end. My poor love.

I gently ease my way out of bed so as not to disturb her too much and head for the kitchen where I have to steal myself not to cry. I can't and daren't go back in the bedroom, I just do not want to see my little girl like this but I know I have to as I need a change of clothes. Quietly I re-enter the room and she doesn't even react and just lays there motionless. I select a change of clothes - it doesn't matter what stupid label they are today as that issue is completely irrelevant - underwear, t-shirt, jeans and trainers and then head to the bathroom.

After a quick shower I fix my hair up as per my usual way and add some light make-up, nothing fancy. I skip breakfast for the second day running, not even having a cup of tea or coffee because I don't want any, I'm just not in the mood for anything.

I ring the vets and get through to Amanda herself directly - fortunately she's on duty once again today - she telling me that it's for the best that I bring Lacey in straight away.

This is probably the single-most hardest thing that I've ever had to do in my life so far and I am both scared and afraid; scared of Lacey's pain and afraid of being left alone.

I go and fetch Lacey's basket and put it down on the bed right next to her and stroke her little head once again, cherishing the moment while I still can. As I attempt to lift her she stiffens and emits the most painful scream imaginable and my heart sinks to the bottom of the ocean. I hold her and gently stroke her fur my poor love, as I try to ease her into her basket.

I want

The journey to the vets feels like the final journey to Heaven and we arrive there all too soon. Amanda is there waiting for us as we walk in and after quiet "Hello's" we enter the examination room.

What follows next requires no title or explanation. It is surreal and peaceful and horrible and cruel all at one and the same time and I just cannot believe this is happening. Myself and Amanda's assistant gently hold Lacey down as Amanda injects the fatal drug into her pre-shaved right-forearm. I stroke her in life and then in death as she slowly slips away from me.

She is gone.

I struggle to believe that that is it; that she has died and left me to my own self? How could she do that? Where do I go from here?

I break down at once and collapse onto the floor in floods of tears, despair and the sheer horror of what I've just done. The girl assistant leaves us and goes back to the reception desk as Amanda tries to console me the best she can. But I don't want fucking consoling - I want my Lacey to be alive and well and everything to back to way it was before. I don't fucking want this shit.

I try to regain my composure and I struggle back onto my feet but I'm then immediately confronted by the sight of Lacey's dead body laying there in front of me on the slab. I reach out and touch her and she's soft and warm but motionless and I sniffle and weep for my little girl. Nothing on this Earth can bring her back now. I hate this fucking World and I also want to die so I can be with her in death, both of us together once again.

Amanda carefully places Lacey's limp and lifeless body back into her basket and quietly tells me that I can use the rear exit of the building to leave instead of having to go through the reception area in front of the waiting owners and their animals. I follow her to the back door, thanking her and shaking her hand in gratitude for the professional and graceful way that she sent Lacey onto a better World.

194

Driving back home I feel nothing but emptiness and pain, the loss of my cat overwhelming and consuming everything that exists on this shitty Planet. I leave Lacey in her basket and place her in the bathroom, shutting the door on her so I can't see her. I've already earmarked a nice little spot in the flowerbed right in front of my parking space that will be perfect for her burial plot. I'll attend to that grim task tonight when it's dark as I don't want the nosey neighbours getting involved in any of my business. They are nothing to me.

I spend the vast majority of the day dragging around my own shadow. The flat is deathly quiet and still. The flat is also dead. I want to drink myself stupid but it would be too disrespectful to Lacey's memory so I stay away from alcohol and all its evilness.

My mobile suddenly rings and it's Mum, checking-up to see if I'm okay? She wants to come over but I say "No". I don't want to see or talk to anyone, not even her; I just want to be left alone to grieve.

And that's what I am now, alone once again. Lacey may have been a cat but she was also my best friend, my only real friend. I already feel lost without her. How long will this grief continue to haunt me I wonder?

It's 10.30pm when I retrieve Lacey from the bathroom and carry her into the living room as it's now time for her to depart my life physically. I've laid-out her favourite blanket on the coffee table as I intend to bury her wrapped in it in her little grave. Placing her basket on the sofa I open its door and slide her out and onto the blanket.

Unwrapping the cover that Amanda put over her Lacey's dead body I look down upon her for the very last time in this mortal life. I struggle to breathe normally as I sit there staring at her lifeless body and when I touch her soft fur I feel my eyes welling-up with yet more tears of sadness.

She lays there frozen, her poor old body now stiff with rigor mortis. I stroke and kiss her but there is no response, she is not of this Earth any longer. I sob a little and I feel so helpless.

What can I do to bring her back to life? It's a stupid and futile question and the answer is easy - nothing. I kiss her one last time on the top of her head and wrap her back up, not forgetting to put her favourite toy mouse in with her for the journey into the next life.

I carry her down to the car park and place her gently down in front of my car. There isn't a single soul around and the air is deathly quiet. It's like this night has been made solely for this solemn purpose. Taking my trowel I dig-away frantically at the earth, desperately trying to hold back my tears as I do so. I dig down some 25cm before I hit several large stones and bricks and can go no further.

I place Lacey in the hole and wish her well - my only friend and love. I touch her through her blanket, stroking her body for the very last time and then she is gone, buried under earth and mud as I scrape it back in the hole over her with flowing tears and all-consuming grief.

After patting the earth down with my bare-hands I stand at her graveside. It's all too much for me to bear and I curse this fucking Planet and everyone on it as I shout at the cool night sky, screaming like a banshee.

Nothing exists anymore - no people, no animals, no buildings, no money, no cars. Nothing except the empty shell that is me.

Back indoors I desperately search the flat for my cat but she's nowhere to be found - not on my bed, not in her sleeping-basket, not on the back of the sofa, nowhere. I know she's dead and gone but she must be here somewhere? In vain desperation I turn for help and guzzle down the last remnants of the vodka, about a quarter of a bottle. I hit the wine next, half a bottle of German white straight from the fridge, followed by several lagers and then the gin.

I am no more.

***

It's 11.30am the following morning when I regain consciousness, my head feels like it has been in a vice and my stomach is in terrible pain. Not only that there's vomit all over the arm of the sofa and down my chest. The pain in my kidneys is excruciating and I have trouble standing up straight as I make my way to the bathroom for a wee and a poo and to clean myself up.

I also notice that it's pouring with rain outside and it beats down on the balcony floor and the glass of the French-doors, making its own music as it does so. I certainly won't be going anywhere today that's for sure.

As I pass my bedroom I notice a small round indentation in my duvet from where Lacey had been asleep, still preserved in time after all these hours have flown by. I hope and pray that she's okay on the other side and is not too scared and that she's found peace in the arms of my Guardian Angel and she'll keep in touch with me with her subconscious subliminal messages from the Spirit World.

Lacey was more than just a cat - she was my friend.

My insides must really be pretty beaten-up as I notice my faeces are a nasty dark colour, almost black like a piece of charcoal. Even so I feel a little better now that I've evacuated, so in the kitchen I switch the kettle on to make myself a mug of sweet tea to try and perk myself up a bit. With the death of Lacey I feel like a phantom of my own self, just wandering around the flat like a figment of my own imagination.

Standing at the balcony doors sipping my tea I watch the World go by below me in the rain. Just what the Hell do these people think they're doing? They're all walking about trapped in their own little World's, totally oblivious to everything that's going on around them, including life and death. Is there any point to life let alone death? We all have our good and bad times and we all have to take the rough with the smooth, but sometimes I just have to ask myself why? What the fuck is it all for?

For me right now, at this very moment, every day is a bonus and I'm not letting anyone stop me in my journey. I can both laugh at my sadness and cry at my good fortune of being alive and being me. Whilst I still have blood pumping through my veins - and admittedly some alcohol! - I will continue to fight to the bitter end.

I decide to go out in the end as I need to do something, and so I find myself at the Garden Centre on the edge of town. My clothes today are a beautiful white cotton blouse, a black mini-skirt and black wool leggings, all from Topshop. On my feet I'm wearing a pair of black suede platform ankle-boots from AXParis and due to the weather, I'm wearing my white cashmere poncho from Peter Hahn which sets off my whole outfit superbly. My underwear is in sexy-red from Victoria's Secret and my perfume is *Poison* by Christian Dior.

I'm here just nosing around looking for some kind-of plaque or stone to place on Lacey's grave. There's lots of resin ones featuring birds and hedgehogs and all that crap, all in bright garish colours, even a few cat ones, but nothing that's really suitable. I head to the stone statue section where I find cherubs, loads of Green Man heads, dogs, naked women and then at long last a few cat sculptures. One of them catches my eye straight away - a sleeping cat all curled-up looking peaceful, made from a pale-yellow type of stone. Its perfect and I have to have it regardless of the price, a not too expensive £20.

On the way home I stop for some petrol at my local station as I'm running a bit low. However, when I arrive I notice a queue of cars has formed at the pumps so I decide to give it a miss and drive on to the next one - a distance of only an extra 3-miles or so. At this one there is virtually no-one there at all, only a couple of cars lined-up at the pumps. I pull up to the next vacant one and go to put £25-worth of petrol in my tank.

As the fuel flows I sense a strange presence surrounding me, like I'm being watched by something evil. I slowly turn my head to the right and see a small shitty old blue Peugeot at the pump directly behind me. Its driver stares at me with the face of death and I stare back at him in pure horror when I notice that its none other than the "Old Man" - my father.

It's the very same look with the same dead eyes that I remember from all those years ago that are boring into me - like the Grim Reaper himself. We just stand there staring at each other for some 30-seconds but it feels considerably longer as he then breaks away, gets back into his car, reverses out of the station and drives away. All this is done without him actually getting any fuel or even saying one single solitary word too me or acknowledging me in any way. Bastard.

I try to prize myself out of my living nightmare but instead I just stand there frozen in total shock. I don't know what to do, say or think. All of a sudden the handle on the fuel-hose starts to click violently and snaps me out of my daze. I then notice that I've accidently put £57-worth of fuel into my tank, way-more than I wanted - fuck it! In the station shop I pay the Asian on the till in cash and then make my way home with my mind numb and cold as I start to throw questions at myself.

Why did that old bastard ignore me? Why didn't he say "Hello"? How can he be like that to his own daughter? What the fuck have I ever done wrong? I bet he doesn't even know he has a Granddaughter let alone what her bloody name is? And what the Hell was he doing around here in the first place; he lives nearly 25-miles away? I hope he dies a long, slow, painful lingering death.

It's still raining as I pull-up in my parking space, the time now being 4.30pm. I squat down and place the stone I bought onto Lacey's grave, the drops of rain turning its colour to a darker shade as it gets totally covered. I stand back and admire my purchase, it's absolutely perfect for her and makes me both smile and sad at the same time. I really miss my baby so much as I stand there wiping away a single tear from my cheek.

Once indoors I try to vodka the event of seeing the "Old Man" out of my mind but it's no use - his death-mask of a face is burned into my eyes forever and I start to sob uncontrollably at my pain. Will I ever be free of that bastard?

This situation is typical of my fate; if the first petrol station hadn't been rammed-full then none of this shit would've happened in the first place. This is how my life is.

That same evening I send an Email to Amanda, thanking her once again for her compassion in my time of need and for all the care she had shown to Lacey in her final days on this Earth.

***

Time has moved on and it's now almost 3-months later and nothing has changed, not one bloody thing. I suppose the one big thing that has actually happened is that Steve is no-longer part of my life. He cheated on me whilst he was in America with another girl, a work colleague. He's back in England now though, in the arms of yet another girl. And good-luck too them, I really mean that, because I always knew that he would cheat on me just as I've cheated on him, not only with the young guy that I met at the supermarket ages ago but with others that I'm not going to tell you about.

This is the madness of life and what its made me into today, trapped in my own little World where no-one can mess with my dreams. I truly believed that Steve was different, that maybe he could even have been "The One", but once again fate intervened and saved me from the shackles of love. It was fate that drove us together and it was fate that drove us apart.

Ever since Lacey passed-away I feel as though my personality has changed, I feel somewhat calmer and mellow, just a little anyway. Her death really did hit me for six and I don't think that I will ever get over it. Out of the darkness and into the light.

Work is also the same, still the same old boring crap with the same old boring people. Rachael left some weeks ago now and has had her baby, a little boy named Max. I haven't seen him yet but she has Emailed me some pics of him and he's so cute I could almost eat him!

I'm sitting at work bored out of my fucking skull, but at least it's almost time for the afternoon tea-break. Suddenly I feel the presence of someone lurking behind me and I catch a quick glimpse of my supervisor Judy out the corner of my eye, trying to attract my attention for some reason? I finish with the customer on the other end of the line and take my headset off and place it around my neck.

"Sarah, would you come with me to my office please." She says in a strange muted manner, talking to me like I've suddenly regressed back into a 6-year old child.

"Why? What's the problem?" I enquire, but all I receive is a sorrowful look in return.

We walk the short distance to her office in silence, closely followed by the usual stares of inquisition from my nosey fellow co-workers. Once there I'm met by "Wingnut" - the boss - and two Police officers, one male and one female.

"Miss Sarah Knowles?" says the youngish female officer, quite attractive and in her late-20's.

"Yes, that's right. What is it? What's happened?" I reply concerned.

"I'm really sorry to have to tell you Miss Knowles that your Mother passed-away earlier this morning."

"What are you talking about? I spoke to my Mum this morning, first thing, about 8-o'clock, just before I set-off for work." I snap back at her, not wanting to believe what she's saying even if it is the truth, whatever that is?

"I'm sorry Miss Knowles, there's no mistake. Apparently your Mother collapsed in the garden and was discovered by one of her neighbours, a Miss Braun. It was her that raised the alarm. Unfortunately when the Paramedics arrived there was nothing they could do. I'm really sorry."

I collapse down in one of the office chairs in pure disbelief. This cannot be happening? It can't be true? Are they taking the piss out of me by playing this sick joke on me? I only spoke to her this morning and she was as fit as a fiddle.

"If you would like, we could take you to the hospital where you could see your Mother." Pipes-up the male officer. He's a lot older than his partner at around 40-ish and has a big round beer-belly.

"Yes. Yes, okay." I say back in shock as I struggle to get to my feet. I am totally numb. This is unreal.

"Take as much time as you need Sarah." Says Judy as she gently touches my arm in what I can only describe as some sort-of "sympathy?"

I head back to my desk to log my computer off and get my things, ignoring everyone around me as they don't exist in my life anyway. I then head out and away with the two officers in the back of their Police car, being scanned all the time by the "plebs".

I am completely in the hands of the officers as we enter the hospital. They automatically seem to know exactly where to go and who to see as they've obviously done this a thousand times before. They must have hearts of stone.

After a quick chat with one of the Doctor's - a short, fat Asian guy with a big round face that looks as though it's about to burst at any second! - followed by condolences and other stuff I don't remember, I'm shown into a side room where I find my sister Kate sitting there in tears along with baby Abigail and the bad-penny that is Kate's so-called "boyfriend" Mick.

After a hug and a kiss to Kate and the baby, we're both shown into an adjoining room, the room that contains our dead Mother, laying there under a thin white sheet. The Doctor folds the sheet back to reveal the cold, ghostly face that is our Mum.

The first thing that hits me is that her mouth is open. That's just typical of her - even in death her mouth is still trying to talk! Only now though there is no sound coming from it. In fact the room itself is in complete silence except from Kate's sobbing.

And from me? There is nothing - no tears, no feeling, nothing at all. Just emptiness and detachment from everything around me. I don't know why I feel like this? Maybe I have no more grief left in me after Lacey's death?

We recover back into the anti-room and after some nonsensical chit-chat and more hugs we all go our separate ways once more. Both Kate and I are fiercely independent women so there's no need to drag it out and embarrass ourselves anymore than we really want to.

The two Police officers offer to take me home so I take them up on their kindness, it's only a short distance away anyway and so we head off once more.

Back in my own little insulated World behind closed doors I pour myself a large neat vodka and take up my usual position on the balcony overlooking the road below, watching all the humans pass by.

The events of the day still haven't sunk in yet and I don't feel they ever will for some reason? My very being somehow feels indistinguishable between life and death and I feel numb and detached from them both. This is all part of the steep learning curve of life. Dying is the easy part; it's the living that's the hard bit.

I sit on the balcony for ages, surprisingly only having a couple of drinks as I'm not really in the mood to get totally pissed out of my head. With Lacey gone and now my Mum I am truly alone. We are all born alone and we all die alone and that's the sad fact.

I find it a little weird that when Lacey died I was overcome with grief but now with Mum's passing I feel nothing. I do feel some loss of course but it's hit me nowhere near as bad as my poor old cat's death. Why? Maybe I have some kind-of delayed shock? Maybe it's a different kind of love that we had between us?

***

I'm off work for the next 6-days on compassionate leave, which of course gives me plenty of free time for my one and only self to think, play and generally do as I bloody-well want. I've started pleasuring myself once again on a more regular basis as I'd stopped completely for some while after Lacey's death as doing it just didn't seem right somehow? It's strange isn't it, the funny things we do?

It's not all free time of course, as there's Mum's funeral to arrange and also the sale of the old family house which I'll be very glad to see the back of. Maybe it will put to rest some of the ghosts and bad memories from times past? Mum's solicitor is taking care of the house sale so at least that's one big headache that's been taken away from Kate and me. He's also helping us with some of the funeral arrangements as part of Mum's will, in which - once the house is sold off - we both get an equal share of the house money as well as the 50-grand in cash that she had squirreled-away somehow? After the solicitor has taken his cut obviously.

Mum's service and cremation is set for the day after tomorrow, with only myself, Kate and baby Abigail as family as there's no-one else left. There are about twenty of Mum's friends invited and a small do afterwards that has been arranged by our old family friend and former neighbour Karen back at the house.

And as for Mum's old cat Suzie? Well, I've taken her in and it's been really strange having another cat wandering around the flat once again, and also quite therapeutic in a way. We seem to get along really well together so it's worked out okay for the both of us on that front. I love her to bits.

***

The day of Mum's funeral came around far too quickly, but at least it all went well enough - as cremations go that is. There's no point in dwelling on all the proceedings and as to what clothes I was wearing and all that crap as it's completely meaningless - it was a funeral so you can draw your own picture and colour it in at the same time.

The one fact is though, all that day, and throughout this whole sorry tale, is that I've shed not one single solitary tear. Why can't I show my inner-self without fear of ridicule and persecution from the arseholes who so openly and freely display theirs?

I did actually come close to weeping though, twice. The first was when we were following behind the hearse in the funeral car driving through Mum's home town. The place was fairly busy with shoppers, some of whom looked at us as we passed by but the majority of them just didn't bother. But there was one guy though – a typical builder-type wearing a yellow hard-hat and one of those day-glow safety jackets and was completely covered in brick dust - who stopped by the edge of the road and took his hat off, placed it over his heart and bowed his head as a mark of respect. It was such a poignant and beautiful gesture from a total stranger and I wanted to jump out of the car there and then and go and hold him in my arms and thank him but you know that I didn't do that of course, we just carried on through.

The second time I nearly lost it was when they played the song *Spirit in the Sky* by Norman Greenbaum at the end of the service, a tune that Mum requested be played in the event of her death. I'm not being nasty, but I don't think I'll be able to listen to that song ever again.

Being back in the old family house without Mum's presence was a bit weird though, especially with all of her friends there and not her. Everyone was really nice and very sympathetic and all that and the day concluded without any hassle. I didn't even make a spectacle of myself by getting bladdered!

Clearing out the house was a real major task, although once again Mum's solicitor helped us a lot and both Kate and I could not have done it so quickly without him; for a price of course - nothing in life or even death is free. Indecently, according to the coroner's report, she had a massive heart-attack, poor old Mum. I really hope that she didn't suffer and that it was all over quickly.

Up in the loft Kate and I found some of our dusty old school books and reports that Mum had stashed away in a cardboard box. Flicking through them was like looking at someone else's life; I couldn't believe it was my work that I was looking at - very surreal! Even though I left school only 16-years ago, I don't really have many memories of it. I never liked it much anyway and couldn't wait to leave. I did have a few friends there but no-one special and I lost contact with those after only 6-months or so. My contemporaries back then were pretty-much nothing and nowhere to me, just as they are now.

Looking back, I was really lost back then, even more so than I am now. This was mainly due to all the problems at home with the "Old Man", but I really don't want to get back onto the subject of him again and open up old wounds. He's dead to me even though he's still alive.

Also I shot my bolt way too early with some of the boys at school and I think that's made me even wearier of settling down with anyone. I'd lost my virginity early at thirteen - up against a tree in the small orchard within the school grounds with one of the older boys. I can't even remember his name!

Going through my old school reports was also a bit strange - were they really talking about me? I received a "C" for average at every subject except for art where I got an "A". I didn't come away from there with much in the way of qualifications, no A or O-Levels or anything like that, just the basics. Not that I've ever needed them anyway as I had already found an office job locally before I had even officially left school. Since that day I've never looked back and why should I? The past is the past.

We also found a collection of Mum's old diaries dating back years. The ones relating to her time with the "Old Man" were too excruciating to read so I hastily put them back down. They made me suddenly recall an event from years ago when I was on the eve of leaving the family home when I stupidly took a look through Mum's then-current diary - I wish I hadn't. There was not one single mention in it about me and all the problems I was going through with "Him" at the time - nothing. There was plenty in there about Kate and the problems she was having at school and all that shit, so why did Mum omit me from her thoughts? What had I ever done to her to warrant exclusion? None of it makes any sense - as per usual.

Mum's house took some 3-months to sell, mainly because of its old-fashioned condition. We had to drop the price in the end by some 20-grand just to get rid of it, which by South of England status is crazy. Eventually it went to an Asian family, a fact that makes me sick to my bloody stomach. If that poor old house could express its emotions it would be of tears and sadness due to all the trauma it has had to endure over the years.

There is one horrible thing that I will always remember for the rest of my life on that peculiar day of the funeral though. When I arrived home that evening I parked my car as per usual in my allotted space, and after getting out I made my usual cursory glance over to Lacey's grave to say "Hello" and there it was - or rather wasn't - as some fucking bastard had stolen her gravestone, the yellow one that I bought at the garden centre a while ago.

How fucking low can these scum go? To say I was angry would be the understatement of the century, I was livid beyond belief. What goes through the minds of these arseholes that they think they can go around just nicking whatever they fucking like?

I made-up some small leaflets on my computer, including my land-line and mobile numbers as well as my Email address, and stuffed them through all my neighbours letter-boxes, asking them if they had seen anyone taking Lacey's stone? It was a complete waste of time; the result was zilch.

One week later however, I received a somewhat sharp letter from my local Council stating:

"Under no such circumstances are you allowed to interfere with Council property by placing statues on Council owned and maintained ground, and on and on and on blah blah fucking blah."

How fucking snotty! Obviously one of my bloody nosey neighbours had grassed me up, the bastards. If I find out who it was there'll be fucking trouble that's for sure.

As far as Mum's ashes were concerned, it was her wish to have them scattered on the hill overlooking Amberley, at the top of Bury Hill in West Sussex. Both Kate and I undertook the solemn task together and once again it was an event that is just bloody typical of the way my life runs.

We poured the contents of her urn out together into the wind only for it to suddenly turn and smack me back in the chops! Do you see what I mean? Even in death she's still in my face!

***

Life goes on and so I've booked Mum's old cat Suzie in for an appointment at the vets this evening to have her yearly booster injection and for a general check-up. I also need to get her details changed over to my name and address as I haven't had time to do it yet.

I'm not going out later dressed to kill either, so I'm just wearing a pink and grey biker t-shirt from Grand Prix Legends, a pair of stone-washed skinny-jeans from New Look and a pair of blue walking-boots from Cotton Traders. My sexy underwear is from Ultimo in pink, with my perfume being *Poison* by Christian Dior. My hair I leave as is, with my make-up being both light and sharp.

To my surprise, Amanda is on duty tonight (doesn't she ever have any time off?) and it's so good to see her once again. At least this time it's in more pleasant circumstances after the horrible trauma of the last time with Lacey. We laugh and chat and talk about life and death and all that crap as she checks Suzie over and gives her the OK, we even agree to meet-up for a drink sometime. When I turn to leave she looks at me and smiles coyly; it seems as though I've found a new friend!

Later that night back at my flat, I'm naked and on all fours, pretending that Amanda is fucking me with my dildo from behind as I press it gently into my vagina. I quickly cum as the plastic phallus parts my lips and internal muscles with both pleasure and pain as I ease it in and out of my hole.

I pant uncontrollably as I imagine licking Amanda all over her tight Australian body and then fucking her with my tongue and fingers. I lay on my back and screw myself with my special friend and cum over it and my hand and then lick it off as I cum for the third time and gently slap my fanny with my right-hand, making me yelp like a big girl - Ha!

I'm almost completely done-for as I stagger into the kitchen and grab myself a half-full bottle of white from inside the fridge door. I guzzle it down as I start to wank myself silly, then repositioning myself on the floor face-up and ease the end of the bottle into my twat with the remainder of its contents partly filling my love-tube with wine and the rest spilling out onto the shinny kitchen floor. Pulling it out I pour the remnants of the wine over my breasts and face and suck on the end of the bottle, pretending that it's Amanda's hard clitoris.

With the bottle empty I drop it over to one side, making Suzie jump as I do so. I pick her up and stroke her with all my love, her moulting fur sticking to my wine-covered skin as I give her a big soppy kiss to her head.

On my computer I Email Amanda, asking her out for that drink she mentioned earlier. I hope my message is coherent enough as my vision is somewhat blurred from the alcohol and my self-pleasuring which I continue to inflict upon myself as I press "Send" and cum.

**

I WANT

In my life at the moment I feel like a blind person standing at a crossroads. And yet I can't even see the bloody road let alone know which way I'm supposed to turn?

I know it sounds a bit clichéd and it is. My life over the past however many years had been one based on pure subterfuge. When I think back about all the shit that I've had to put up with in my life over the years, I wonder how the Hell I've survived it all?

I really do hope that one day I will find my utopia, and then the whole World had better watch out because I will have more power that any God can wield.

The World is already full of damaged souls and I know that I'm one of them, but that doesn't mean I'm going to dig my own grave. I intend to live and fight to my last breath and no bastard is going to get in my way; whatever the outcome.

***

It's 7.30pm on Thursday evening. I've just finished having dinner and I'm now sitting at my computer checking my Emails. There's yet more moaning from Kate about her usual boring pet subjects - the baby crying, Mr. Useless, lack of sleep blah blah blah blah blah. It's a never-ending story of mind-numbing crap.

Hidden amongst the usual detritus is the return Email from Amanda, telling me that she would love to meet-up for a drink but the only free time she has is this coming Saturday lunchtime due to the rota that she's on at the vets.

I send her a reply message saying Saturday would be okay and asking her if she wants to meet up at my local pub, The Cricketers, at 1pm and that it would be really great if she could make it.

She returns with her confirmation straight away, adding "Love" and an "X" at the end of her message.

My stomach churns as to where this might lead, and I wonder to myself if I've been reading too much into our budding little friendship?

***

For a Saturday I'm up reasonably early at 9am. After breakfast of tea and toast I shower, do my hair and add my full-on power make-up. I'm going for a 1950's-style American look today with a classy white vintage blouse and a tight white knee-high pencil-skirt - both from Monshowroom - that buttons-up at the back and really shows-off my curves. On my feet I'm wearing my favourite shoes once again - you know very well which ones! - as I love them to bits. My perfume is *Mademoiselle* by Chanel.

Amanda's already at the pub when I arrive at 12.45pm which takes me a little by surprise as I really like to be in pole-position and not come second. She looks really pretty, dressed in a white blouse - not as nice or as expensive as mine obviously! - a pair of blue stone-wash jeans and white trainers.

"Hi Sarah, you look nice." She exclaims as our eyes meet. I look fucking amazing let alone "nice" I think to myself, cheeky cow!

She gets the first round in - a large neat vodka for me, which when I take a sip is obviously watered-down - and a gin and tonic for herself. We go and sit ourselves down outside in the pub garden, it being such a lovely warm day it would be a waste not to take full advantage of it. We chat and laugh about stuff - work, the weather, clothes, Australia, men – I guess I must be wrong about the signals then? - and life in general.

After a couple more rounds of drinks, Amanda invites me back to her flat with the pretext of her showing me some photos and stuff of her native Australia. Of course I say "Yes", what the fuck do you think I was going to say?

We take her car - a Japanese rat-box that I wouldn't give 100-quid for! - and off we go. Her flat is only a few miles from mine and is located above one of the shops in the High Street which is handy, albeit a bit too noisy for my liking. Her flat is really nice inside, although not finished to the high standard of my own, and is dominated by a gigantic print of Ayres Rock hanging on the main feature wall. How very Australian!

We sit ourselves down next to each other on the sofa with a glass of white wine each - Australian of course! - as Amanda shows me pictures from her past in a giant black photo album. Australia is such a massive country that I cannot really comprehend the sheer size of it, it really is huge, and beautiful also. She shows me photos of her family and friends back home, shots of her home town of Stirling in South Australia in the Adelaide Hills, with its beautiful red-leafed Autumn trees and old colonial houses.

There are also some pictures of ex-boyfriends, family pets and other stuff, including her time at veterinary training at Bristol University in South West England.

The following 2-pages contain some photos of her with another girl, very similar-looking to her in fact - blonde, slim and pretty - who I imagine at first is her younger sister, but when I enquire Amanda shyly tells me that the girl in question was in fact her girlfriend at the time when she was at vet school. That is girlfriend as in "girlfriend" - you know what I mean?

Oh well, here we go again!

"Sarah, you know that I'm attracted to you don't you?" She asks me, looking straight at me with those big beautiful round eyes of hers.

"Well, yes, I did get that impression." I reply with a little reservation in my voice.

"I was hoping that you might feel something for me? I think you're absolutely beautiful." She says in her sweet Aussie tone as she looks at me wantonly.

"I'm guessing that you're not attracted too me?" she continues.

"No, it's not that. I just didn't really think that you felt that way about me." I say.

Without another word she leans closer to me and I to her and we kiss one soft kiss to each other and it's glorious. We pull-back momentarily as she touches my hand with hers and I lean forward and kiss her soft lips once again, enjoying her taste on my mouth.

I move closer to her and with my left-hand I touch her right-breast, sensing its size and firmness. She sighs breathlessly as I squeeze her and she moves closer and kisses me hard, flicking her tongue in and out of my mouth as she does so. I feel her hand move to my waist and then slowly up to my boobs which she fondles and squeezes, making me gasp in excitement. Oh fucking Hell!

We French-kiss in passion as I push my hand between Amanda's legs, making her breathing skip a beat as I finger her vagina through her clothes.

She leans back and slowly removes her blouse, revealing her lovely round breasts contained within a white lacy bra. I too remove mine and throw it to the floor to join hers as she then moves-in to kiss my peaches, running a rivulet of saliva over them with her tongue.

Amanda stands and removes her jeans, tossing them to one side over the end of the sofa, and then doing the same with her bra. Moving closer I kiss her naked mounds as I run my fingers between her legs once more, only this time the sensation on her twat is far greater through the thinner material of her knickers and she moans loudly as I feel the wetness of her vulva.

Rising to my feet I reveal my totally naked self to her, my perfect body in all its splendour as she removes her knickers to expose her beautiful shaved slot. We embrace and kiss like lovers do, the emotion overpowering the both of us as we become engulfed in each other's lust.

I lay back on the sofa as Amanda squats-down before me and eases my legs apart. I beg her to "Lick my pussy like a bitch" as I suddenly feel her mouth and tongue make contact with my labia. I fly up to Heaven as she kisses and laps at my twitching quim, firing my serotonin impulses and making me orgasm and cum at her in seconds.

We swop-over positions, with Amanda on her knees and leaning on the sofa as I kiss and lick at her bum-cheeks as I finger-fuck her vagina. She screams in spasticated pleasure and cums on my hand as we love. We both climb on the sofa together and make love like two lovers should - soft and tender and with gentle care for each other's wants and needs.

We remain in each other's arms seemingly for ages, not wanting to be the first to let the other go. Finally we move to the floor and 69 each other with me on the bottom and Amanda on top as we lick-away at each other's vaginas. In under a minute she cums on me and screams as I tongue her harder, lapping at the soft rubbery texture of her clit and drinking-down her honey.

She pulls my lips apart and kisses my clit hard, instantly making me spit at her as we love and roll around on the floor, laughing and enjoying the thrill of being two beautiful naked women exploring each other in totality as we fuck.

We're both a little done-for and we sit and talk and laugh and joke and touch and kiss. I tell Amanda of my love with young Jennifer last year and how I shocked myself with my actions with her, but with Amanda this feels different somehow? It just feels so right and we kiss and touch each other intimately as we giggle and laugh like girls.

Time is quickly moving on and Amanda has to get ready for work as she's on the evening shift at the vets tonight. We shower together, kiss, dry each other's bodies, finger, and then dress each other, embrace and then kiss more.

I go to leave and we kiss and tongue as Amanda takes me to her car. She drives me back to the pub in order for me to collect my car and we sit and talk and laugh and hold hands before we part with a long passionate full-on kiss.

We both promise to call each other and as I start to walk over to my car I feel a small tear form in the corner of one eye in sadness of our parting. I don't want to walk away; I want to be with my new lover forever. I turn and run back to her, back around to Amanda's side of the car and we kiss one another again with love through her open window as I touch one of her breasts and fall madly in love with her.

I love her totally with all my heart and I desperately want us to be together forever. I'm completely lost to her from this moment on.

***

I know I've said this a thousand times before, but as time moves on we all change. Things that happen to us dictate to a large degree who we are today, especially from the effects and actions of other people. These things leave scars that are hard and sometimes impossible to heal, you only have to analyse your narrator for living proof of that!

It may be a fact that I think too much, or that I have an over-fertile imagination, who knows? The upshot is that we all need some kind-of love, whether it's emotional or physical or a mixture of both, without either we are all lost souls.

Changes are coming; I just know they are, I can feel it.

***

I arrive at work at my usual time. It's Wednesday and I've had the previous 2-days off just to chill-out and stuff.

Today I look like a ghost. I'm wearing a white Bodycon dress from BooHoo with matching white lace underwear from Ultimo. I'm also bare-legged and have my fave blue Lola heals on once again. I've gone for a simple look to my make-up featuring pale-pink lipstick and coal-black eye-shadow which all together makes me look like I have the face of death! My perfume is *Opium* by Yves Saint Laurent.

I sense a strange air about the place as I make my way to my desk, sit my perfect arse down and turn my computer on.

"What's going on?" I whisper across to Thelma.

"Thirteen people were made redundant yesterday." Comes back her shock reply.

"You're joking me? Who's gone then?" I say.

She lists out some names of the ones that have departed - some I know and some I don't - and its right across the board, throughout every department, including my own with the loss of Jennifer, my little lesbian friend in the corner. I sit there in shock and I really feel sorry for her - my poor little Jen.

Just as I'm about to put my headset on and take my first call of the day, Judy the department supervisor, breezes up to me.

"Sarah, I don't need you on the phones today, there are some special orders that need collating and inputting before the end of the month, that's by tomorrow afternoon, so I need you to do those first okay?" She bitches at me.

Did you get all that? No "Good morning" or "Did you have a nice couple of days off?" or any of that shit. Not even a mention about the poor sods that got the chop yesterday, i.e. Jennifer. The selfish old cow.

The collating job is a right bastard to do although it's something that I've done a few times before. What I don't understand though is why the big rush all of a sudden? Even so I get stuck into it straight away and the day whizzes by pretty quickly and it's soon time to knock-off and escape out of this shit-hole.

That evening I have a strange sense of foreboding, an almost empty feeling I guess, that makes my stomach turn over in not a very nice way. What the Hell is that all about? Maybe it's the sudden departing of my special friend little Jen?

I hit the sack early at 9.50pm.

***

Before long it's Thursday morning and today I'm wearing a stylish yellow jumper from Looxent, a pair of tight grey-coloured stonewash jeans from Topshop and a beautiful pair of knee-high black suede boots from Farfetch that are a bit over-the-top for work but I don't care; I look bloody amazing in them so that's all there is to it! My underwear is from Agent Provocateur in sexy red lace while my perfume is *Luxe* by

Avon. By my reckoning, I should just about get all the collating done by late-afternoon at a push and then I can piss-off out of here and into freedom.

I plug-away all bloody day on this soul-sucking crap, when finally at 4.30pm its all done and dusted and I sign it off finished. I'm a little bit knackered by now so I decide to go for a quick wee in order to kill some time before leaving.

I return to my desk after only some 10-minutes or so to find Judy hovering around it like a bloody vulture about to strike.

"Sarah, Mr. Wingate would like to see you in his office straight away please." She hurriedly informs me as she then scoots-off before I even have a chance to ask her "Why?"

What the Hell is up now I ask myself? A sudden meta-dark wave of cold expectation freezes my entire body as I walk up to "Wingnuts" office. I knock once on the already open door and ask to come in.

I find "Wingnut" sitting there with his ashen face looking at me like a rabbit caught in the headlights of an oncoming car. He asks me to come in and to shut the door behind me and then to take a seat.

"I guess you realize why I've called you in to see me Sarah?" he says in his usual boring mono-tone voice.

"Is there something wrong with my data-inputting?" I enquire with all the innocence of a little girl lost.

"No, no, it's nothing like that. I'm sorry Sarah, but I'm afraid we have to let you go." He bleats at me.

"What do you mean your letting me go? You're sacking me?" I scream back at him.

"No, we're not sacking you, we're making you redundant. The company has to make cuts in all departments and unfortunately your job is one of them." He informs me coldly, just like a fucking robot.

"But why me? Why not that lazy cow Joan or that fucking Polish bitch or those black bastards in the shipping department? Why me?" I holler back at him.

"There's no need for racist talk Sarah." He whines back.

"What do you fucking mean racist? You don't know the fucking meaning of the word. Everyone in the whole World is racist or haven't you noticed?" I stab at him like a knife.

"I'm sorry Sarah, but the decision has already been made. I have to ask you to clear your desk of any personal items that you may have before you leave. There will obviously be a substantial redundancy package considering the amount of time that you've been with the company and we'll send that on to you in due course along with your P45, a good reference and any other necessary documents." He informs me as cold as ice.

I just sit there in total shock and I'm seething-mad at the same time. Fully steamed-up I let him have it with both-barrels as I jump to my feet, pointing and screaming back at him.

"So what about all that work I've been doing for the last couple of days? That fucking bitch Judy pushed me to get it finished by this afternoon and then I'm kicked out the fucking door half-an-hour later, that's taking the fucking piss. How dare you fucking treat me like this after all the fucking hard work and loyalty I've given to this company."

I lean forwards onto "Wingnuts" desk and hiss in his pasty-white Masonic face and in no uncertain terms give it to him again:

"Let's get one thing absolutely crystal bloody clear. If you fucking think this is the end of me then you're fucking mistaken you old cunt."

"Sarah, I don't know anything about the inputting being completed by today." He bleats back but I cut him off sharply.

"You fucking liar, that fucking bitch Judy knew all along and you expect me to believe that you didn't? If this is the way I'm going to be treated by this fucking company after 7-years service then I don't want to be any part of it, you can all fuck off. And how dare you fucking talk to me like this? You haven't got a fucking clue, none of you. Not one of you knows what living is, you're all fucking brain-dead, the lot of you. You can all kiss my fucking arse."

With that final outburst I turn on my heals and fling "Wingnuts" office door open so hard that it swings back and punches the stud-wall with a dull crashing thud. I make my way to that fucking bitch Judy's office to have it out with her as well only to find it stone-cold empty. In fact the whole fucking department is completely deserted as it's now way past home-time and everyone has clocked-off and gone home. Bastards.

Back at my desk I collect my bag and my one and only personal item - a silver-framed photo of Lacey - and walk out, not even bothering to clock-off as there's no point, I don't work here anymore.

I drive home in a daze. In fact I don't even remember driving home at all as I'm so full of rage. How I keep doing this without ever fucking hitting anything I'll never know? Once safely back at my flat I throw my bag and things onto the sofa without a care, kick-off my heals and hit the vodka.

Suzie has already run for cover, sensing my evil mood, and has hidden herself under my bed for safety.

I'm so fucking angry at being treated this way. Why does this shit always happen to me? I want to shout and scream at someone but there's no-one here to aim my venom at. There's no point in ringing Kate, she's got her own problems and is about as compassionate as a brick anyway. I decide to ring Amanda but there's no answer to her mobile - she must be at work I'm guessing? - so I just leave a tearful message on her voice-mail.

So this is the situation then is it? Fucking redundant at thirty-three? And what a horrible word that is - redundant. I have a feeling of total uselessness and I want to die right here and now but I know that I have more life left in me than to just give it all up because of this stupidity. This is life. You get rid of one problem only for more shit to spring up in its bloody place.

My phone suddenly rings and it's Amanda, and we cry down the line to each other as I tell her that I need her here right now to hold me in her arms to stop me falling apart.

A good half-an-hour goes by before Amanda arrives at my door and I'm in a mess. I don't know how much I've drunk on the slippery slope to oblivion but I feel like shit. We kiss a quick kiss and hold each other as I cry on her shoulder like a baby.

My phone rings again for the second time and it's Rachael, calling to say that she's heard about me being let go - how the fuck did she find out so quickly? She tells me that I'm better off without those twats anyway and that I'll be alright, something will come up, it always does.

I'm so happy with the support of my two best friends - yes, I actually have two friends! - that I sob uncontrollably into Amanda's beautiful embrace.

***

I ease my strap-on dildo in and out of Amanda's vagina and in a matter of only a minute or so she starts to shake wildly and cums for me and it squelches. I pull out of her and we laugh together as we cuddle and love and kiss.

She removes my rubber cock and licks my pie, slowly at first and then harder, using her fingers to open me apart, forcing her tongue deeper into my hole and I cum my cream over her mouth and we are both in rapturous love.

We use my long purple double-ended dildo from Ann Summers on each other as we lay on the living-room floor, inserting either end of its phallic shape into each other's rectal passages. We pump and writhe together in both pleasure and pain and it hurts a little but we ignore it and push.

Both spent, Amanda stands over me like a primeval naked Goddess, her beautifully smooth Australian body glistening from her heat as she moves her body to the motion of sex. Her hair is matted from all the sweat and her eyes are wide and wild with the vision of my fully spread legs and the gorgeousness of my oyster between.

She sprays over me her mixture of urine and cum-juice and I orgasm and cum myself as her mess splashes down on my fanny.

***

It's now 6-months later and both time and my life have moved-on considerably. It took me about 12-weeks to find another job, a lot less than some people I suspect? I'm so glad I was born and raised in the South of England and not in the North where times are a lot harder of that I'm sure.

Unfortunately I had to sign-on at the Job Centre between jobs. To say it was a depressing experience would be the understatement of the bloody century, sitting there amongst the great unwashed waiting to be interviewed by some disinterested mechanical non-entity just so I could receive my sixty-odd quid cheque every week. What they fucking thought I was supposed to do with that bloody insulting amount I don't know? Obviously I would have received more but I don't have a brown face or speak with a Slavic tongue.

Being unemployed did leave me with a great amount of time on my hands for some soul-searching of course. All the preceding years have taken their toll on my mind and body and have left me exhausted and disillusioned about life, my future and even my very existence.

But now I'm back and working for a major insurance company in Horsham, West Sussex. The money is way better than the last company, as are the facilities, so it's all worked out quite well in the end. The people here are exactly the same eclectic simpleminded mix as the last place though, with the usual protagonists - even the bosses - as they are in every establishment. Every company I've ever worked for has been exactly the fucking same - the management do not give a fucking shit about the workers. It's a sad fact but true.

Talking of work, I did receive a cheque for the sum of £6,500 as a pay-off from the old company, plus - surprisingly - a really good reference from old "Wingnut" himself, even though I did call him a cunt! I still feel very hurt by the way I was treated by them in the end of course, keeping me hanging on a bit of string for 2-days just to do their shitty job and then sacking me. I won't forgive or forget that in a hurry that's for sure, I will have my revenge. What comes around goes around.

I've always worked hard for all my employers, something that over the years has back-fired on me as they then all eventually begin to take advantage of my commitment and good-nature. It was inevitable I was going to leave that old company anyway, sooner or later, as I'm far too creative to be chained-up like that. I have so much to do in my life that I need more freedom than any full-time stifling job can provide for me.

Exactly the same can be said of this new job, I won't stay here, I can't, I don't have time. My future awaits me.

I guess the really big news though is that Amanda has moved-in with me and we are now living together as lovers. I know this may come as a bit of a shock to some of you but in reality it couldn't be more right, we really are both deeply in love with each other. I just want someone to love and who will love me back, so what if it's with another girl?

Don't get me wrong though, I'm not gay. I suppose I could be classed as bisexual as I still like cock but I also like pussy as well! Who I choose to have in my bed - male or female - is nothing to do with anyone. I'm a young woman who loves sex, so what? I am eye-candy for both men and women as I've always told you and that suits me just fine. I can have the best of both Worlds.

When I told you that Amanda and I now live together, it's not in the same flat that I had before. That was sold-off several months ago and we have a new one now in the small village of Slinfold in West Sussex which we bought between us using the money from my share of the sale of my flat and the old family home along with Amanda's savings. Amazingly, we now find ourselves completely mortgage free, which is a bit of a result for us at our young age so I think we can count ourselves pretty lucky.

To be honest it was a bit of a wrench to leave Surrey for West Sussex. After all, I was born and have lived there all my life so far, and also worked there exclusively as well. But Surrey has changed for me personally; its become too crowded for one thing and has turned into another satellite of London. So it was time to say "Goodbye" and start afresh in a new County and I haven't looked back.

I still weep tears of sadness over the loss of my beautiful cat Lacey and the melancholy of the whole event still hangs over me. Even though she's gone she will always be here with me - in my heart and in my mind. It was heartbreakingly sad to leave her there in the ground but I couldn't bring her with me, it just wouldn't have been right - my precious love. Before we moved out, there was one important ritual that I just had to perform - to visit her grave one last time, just to say "Farewell" and

"Good Luck" to my special old friend.

Amanda also found herself a new job with another veterinary practice locally as well, so everything has slotted together nicely, thank you for asking! Her parents back in Australia were quite shocked at our getting together I think, a lot more than she's let on I'm sure. Although they're not totally convinced I'm hoping that they've kind-of come around to it. It is her life after all so get over it.

Being with Amanda, I can honestly say that I've never been happier than I am now. And as for her? She seems happy as well and we've made a nice home for ourselves here, along with Mum's old cat Suzie of course. You just never know where life will lead do you?

We will be together for all eternity, buried in each other's arms as we watch every morning's sunrise light up our love.

Not everyone was happy with Amanda's and my chosen path naturally. Kate just doesn't understand and hasn't spoken to me for months, but that's her problem not mine. She also went and had baby Abigail Christened in what was supposed to be a family event but I wasn't invited so therefore I didn't go. Personally I think it was all a waste of money anyway as being a non-believer I just can't see the bloody point? I mean, what is it all about? None of it is fucking real in the first place, and all these fucking morons swallowing this crap are just fooling themselves. It even causes more problems than it solves, including more deaths in the World than any war. Why?

My old friend Rachael was also quite shocked at my news at first but she seems fine with it now. Incidentally, the last time we chatted she told me that my ex-employers are in some sort-of financial trouble and that all the directors and managers have had their company cars taken back to cut costs - what a fucking shame! Bastards. It's no more than they fucking deserve, especially after the way they treated me at the end.

My new work colleagues didn't batter an eyelid when I told them that I swing both ways and that I live with my girlfriend. I guess the Worldview has changed a lot over the years.

All my friends weren't bothered either; simply because I don't have any. In order to be popular one has to conform and that isn't something I intend doing - ever.

I can't say that I've ever had much notion of having children either, and fortunately Amanda feels pretty-much the same. The idea of bringing another life into this cruel World when it's in such turmoil is just ridiculous; it just wouldn't be fair on the child.

Since living together, my little drinking habit has also changed. I still go a bit crazy-bonkers now and then - in fact we both do sometimes as it spices things up, especially when we're making love - but I'm nowhere near as bad as I used to be. I know I would sometimes go overboard with the drink but I was never a bloody alcoholic, although I do admit that there's no telling as to what damage all that binging has done to my precious body. My liver will probably let me know in the future.

Now though, a few drinks after work or at the weekend or when Amanda and I make love is my release from the pressures of life, the pressures of existing in today's World. I really don't need it now like I used to, I guess I've just lost the taste for it I suppose?

As I've already said, I've never been happier than when I'm with Amanda, she is my whole World. Without her I am truly nothing. Happiness is security, and I pretty much have that with her, Suzie, my job, my money, my health and my general well-being. My mental instability, inherited from the "Old Man" - the one that used to call himself my "Father" - is now also much more under control, thanks to my iron-will and sheer bloody-mindedness. It's taken a bloody long time to get to this state of well-being but I know deep down that I'm only a knife-edge away from slipping back into the pit of despair.

I never planned my relationship with Amanda of course, it just happened out of nowhere. Isn't fate a strange companion? And since we've been together I haven't been quite as stressed-out as I used to be, especially after the deaths of both Lacey and Mum. She's bought some stability to my life and I love her for it. I'm still the same passive-aggressive girl on the inside - that will never change of course! - but Amanda has calmed me down a bit. I still have my rants and raves about life and stuff - who doesn't? - but I'm nowhere near as neurotic as I was.

Amanda knows how to calm me down, in her own special way, and I don't just mean with a stiff vodka! Sometimes we just hold each other naked, just embracing each other's skin. It's so pure and beautiful and we are in total and complete love.

***

The Earth is nothing in the Universe. Nothing in the World exists. We as humans are nothing on this Planet, just mere specks.

There is no respect or morals in this World today. Everything and everyone is totally corrupt.

If there's something in my life that I want, I will strive to get it and no-one and nothing is going to stop me. Give me one good bloody reason why I shouldn't? It's my life and I'll do what I like with it. If anyone doesn't like my lifestyle then that's their problem. I will do whatever I want and that's all there is to it. It has nothing to do with anyone else on this Planet how I live my life.

I don't need forgiveness from anyone; I didn't ask to be brought into this fucking World in the first place. I'm not going to conform to any society ideals as no rule-book on life exists. I've worked bloody hard and have suffered for everything that I posses, so why should I be pilloried for living my life my own way? I'm a free woman and at the end of the day I don't have to answer to anyone. Not even my love.

I intend to continue with my supercilious bearing come what may, and if you think I have a mercenary attitude then that's because we live in a mercenary World. I'm not an ego-centric control freak, I just know what I want and I'm determined to get it.

I don't really have any resentment for anyone (except maybe those spoilt little rich kids that have never done a day's fucking work in their puny little insular lives, I can't fucking stand them!) and we all have our own lives to lead of course, whatever they may be? We all have to make the most of what we're given - the rough and the smooth.

We all have an element of *Schadenfreude* within us so what's wrong with that? Other people playing with one's mind can lead to self-destruction and if I've got an attitude then that's because of other peoples attitudes towards me and not necessarily my personality that is the cause and effect - it's as simple as that.

Over time, throughout my life, I have learned how to suffer pain. Through the good times and the bad, and it never ends until our final breath is exhaled.

We all evolve and change accordingly as our lives move on. That is the law of nature and there's nothing you can do about it. Life is a gift from nature that must not be abused.

One day I will find my Satori.

Right here, right now, I am at peace. Things are pretty cool and my outlook is optimistic to say the least. I've got myself a new love and a new job, but I damn-well know that it can all come crashing down on me in seconds at any given moment.

No matter whatever I do I keep coming back to the same conclusion - that is to cut myself off from everyone around me and do my own thing. I know what I want in life and how to get it. This is why I live my life the way I do and no-one is going to stop me in my quest for what I want.

Lightning Source UK Ltd.
Milton Keynes UK
UKOW01f2343160817
307459UK00001B/30/P